MEDJUGORJE:

The Queen of Peace and Her Messages to the World

Includes interviews with visionaries, pilgrims' testimonies, miracles, and the Virgin Mary's final messages.

Anna Garavitt

I dedicate this book to my family (my mother, my brother and my sisters in the convent), whom I love deeply and who have motivated me to continue writing day after day.

Thank you for taking the time to read this book. I have prepared it with much dedication and hope that your faith will be strengthened.

Give your review here:

https://www.amazon.com/review/create-review/edit?ie=UTF8&channel=glance-detail&asin=B0CW6D7ZW4

If you liked my book, it is very important to me that you leave a review on Amazon. It will help me reach more people.

Thank you so much. I pray for all my readers every day.

Sincerely,

Sister Anna Garavitt

Index

Introduction

Dear reader, first of all I would like to thank you for buying my book. I would like to begin by telling you more about myself and my literary inspirations. My name is Anna Garavitt, I was born in Lisbon, Portugal into a very Catholic family, I attended a private Catholic school and my education included religious studies.

I have been a nun for six years. Before that I lived with my mother and my brother, whom I love very much and miss very much, I see them occasionally and they are part of my inspiration for writing.

For many years I have been reading many books, which I have accumulated in my bookshelf, and today I have a collection of more than two thousand literary works. My favorite books are those written in the 80's and 90's about various apparitions of the Virgin Mary around the world and accounts of various visionaries.

However, I have always been a non-believer because I did not discover God's love until certain extraordinary things happened to me that strengthened my faith and made me begin to write with great devotion to God.

I have written several essays, analyses and texts in which I have summarized the most important information from various apparitions, all because I have become a very devout woman since I have had the experience of discovering the love of God and of the Virgin Mary.

For many years I kept all my writings in storage and they were just gathering dust, but I decided to share them with the world because there is no reason or sense to keep them archived. There is a lot of information that is unknown to many authors, but when you read so much, you realize that there are different truths and they all complement each other.

I hope my publication can fill you with peace, love of God, fascination and desire to learn more about this subject, as it did me more than ten years ago.

I have divided this book into several chapters, beginning with the position of the Catholic Church, then with information about the apparitions and the visionaries, then with some reflections on the prayers of some Catholic priests who have a strong and personal connection with Medjugorje, and finally with the experiences of some pilgrims and the latest messages that Our Lady has sent us on the 25th of each month.

I would also like to tell you that this is my first publication on Amazon, I have done my best to make it as understandable as possible and I have enjoyed every second of it. My goal in writing is to strengthen the faith of many people.

At the end of the book, I will leave you with the bibliography that I used at the time to supplement this book. I hope we can meet again in one of my other publications.

CHAPTER 1: POSITION OF THE CATHOLIC CHURCH

In this first chapter, I will present the issues related to the position of the Catholic Church and its evolution over the years. After all, pilgrimages have been approved and each of the Holy Fathers who have been at the head of our Church have been part of these revelations that have taken place in our world.

1.1   MESSAGE FROM FR. RENÉ LAURENTIN

The messages of these apparitions always reflect the message of Jesus Christ in the light of current world conditions. They are meant to inspire us to change, to strengthen and renew our faith, our prayer and our relationship with God. Mary, who was taken body and soul to heaven, is perhaps the most important call in the divine plan to remind us of the need to live the Gospel and keep our faith strong. This is the main task of a true mother, the task of the Heavenly Mother, Mary. These constant apparitions and their messages are the continuous melody of the heavenly symphony, with its infinite and profound variations on a single theme: God's care for His creation and, above all, for humanity.

"It is a mistake to think that we should wait for the approval of the Church before taking an interest in these apparitions or making pilgrimages. If no one were to go to these places where the divine is manifested, the Church would not even have reason to be concerned or to pass judgment on the matter".
– Fr. René Laurentin, renowned theologian and historian of apparitions.

1.2   APPROVAL OF THE CATHOLIC CHURCH

Initially, in December 2017, Archbishop Hoser, Pope Francis' envoy to Medjugorje, reported that the Holy See would allow the organization of official pilgrimages, meaning that dioceses and other institutions could do so without any problems.

In May 2019, the Holy See will officially authorize these pilgrimages. This approval was confirmed during the five-day Youth Festival in August 2019, when pilgrims and Catholic clergy will gather in Medjugorje.

1.3   MEDJUGORJE AND JOHN PAUL II

Pope John Paul II expressed his appreciation for Medjugorje on several occasions. He encouraged people to visit the place, saying that there they experienced conversions, prayed, went to confession, and practiced penance and fasting.

In private conversations, the Pope expressed his desire to visit Medjugorje and asked the faithful to protect him. He also prayed daily for a favorable outcome of these events.

The Pope always emphasized the importance of peace and spirituality and encouraged devotion to the Blessed Virgin Mary. Even after his death, letters were discovered in which he referred affectionately to Medjugorje and thanked those who kept him informed about the events there.

Below are some of the most important dates and events that John Paul II experienced in relation to the events of Medjugorje:

1.   1984: Pope John Paul II affirms to Bishop Paul Maria Hnilica that "Medjugorje is the continuation of Fatima".

2.   1986: In June, the Pope responds to a group of twelve Italian bishops, encouraging them to allow people to visit Medjugorje, where they experience conversions, pray, confess, do penance and fast.

3.   1986 (April 2): In a meeting with Fr. Ivan Dugandzie, O.F.M., the Pope expresses that he is closely following the events in Medjugorje and is praying daily for a favorable conclusion.

4.   1989 (August 1): The Pope speaks to a group of Italian doctors about the importance of the supernatural and how many find it in Medjugorje through prayer, penance and fasting.

5.   1990: During a conversation in February, the Pope mentions that Medjugorje is a great center of spirituality.

6.   1989 (April 21): The Pope says that if he were not Pope, he would already be in Medjugorje, after he was reprimanded for not stopping there on his way back to Rome from Moscow.

7.   1992 (July 20): The Pope urges Fr. Jozo Zovko to take care of Medjugorje and to persevere in it.

8.   1994:   The   Archbishop   of   Paraguay, Monsignor Felipe Santiago Bentez, asks the Holy Father for his approval of the faithful gathered in the spirit of Medjugorje, and the Pope replies: "Approve everything that has to do with Medjugorje.

1.4   THE ROLE OF BENEDICT XVI

After the death of John Paul II, Pope Benedict XVI took an active part in the study of the Medjugorje phenomenon. On March 17, 2010, the Information Office of the Holy See announced the establishment of an International Commission of Inquiry on

Medjugorje, chaired by Cardinal Camillo Ruini. The Commission consisted of six Cardinals, including Cardinal Ruini, the Prefect of the Congregation for the Causes of Saints, Josef Tomko, Vinko Puljic (Archbishop of Sarajevo), Josip Bozanic (Archbishop of Zagreb), and Julian Herranz (President Emeritus of the Pontifical Council for Legislative Texts), as well as a group of theologians and experts in Mariology.

Over the years, the Commission met with all the visionaries in Rome, holding its meetings in a room of the Congregation for the Doctrine of the Faith, where the archives of the Working Group were protected. The commission, according to Fr. Federico Lombardi, the Vatican's press secretary, had a study and research role, without the authority to make definitive decisions or pronouncements. Its function was to offer the results of its study and its opinion, which would be forwarded to the Congregation for the Doctrine of the Faith. The latter would be responsible for making decisions and deciding whether or not to issue a public statement.

Cardinal Camillo Ruini, President of the Commission, stated a few weeks before the resignation of Benedict XVI, on January 11, 2013, that there was still time to complete the investigation of Medjugorje. He expressed that the Consultative Commission would give its opinion, which would be sent to the Congregation for the Doctrine of the Faith, and that the Congregation would decide whether or not to make a public statement. These were the last public statements in this regard before the resignation of Benedict XVI on February 28, 2013, at which time the results of the commission became the responsibility of the new pontiff.

1.5   POPE FRANCIS AND MEDJUGORJE

Since the election of Pope Francis on March 13, 2013, there have been no further official statements from the Vatican regarding Medjugorje. The lack of official statements means that the situation remains inconclusive, especially as the apparitions continue. Although there is no definitive information, it is known that Cardinal Bergoglio, before becoming Pope Francis, closely followed the events in Medjugorje.

As Archbishop, Pope Francis authorized and facilitated the visionary Ivan to give his testimony in Buenos Aires, one of his last decisions before leaving for Rome to be elected Pope. In addition, he received Fr. Jozo Zovko on his missionary visit to Argentina, and in February 2012 he welcomed Fr. Danko Perutina, well known to Medjugorje pilgrims and associated with the spreading of Mary's message in America. Pope Francis also had a short interview with him at the airport of Ezeiza.

CHAPTER 2: ABOUT FACTS AND VISIONARIES

In this second chapter, I will tell you about the most important events that happened in Medjugorje, as well as some facts about the visionaries. From my heart, there were several things that struck me very much. First of all, the experiences of Jackov and Vicka, which arouse a lot of fascination in me, and I would like to go deeper into them. Secondly, the public apparitions of the Virgin Mary, and thirdly, the different motives for prayer of each of the visionaries, which seem to me to have been influenced by the messages of the Virgin Mary in a completely different way, which made them pray for different reasons.

Something that also has a great impact on me are the three notebooks that Vicka wrote about the history of the Virgin Mary, which I hope will one day be revealed and we will be able to know more about our good Mother and in this way increase the faith of the whole world.

2.1 IMPORTANT DATES

June 24, 1981: Prelude to the first apparition. The visionaries see Our Lady from a distance (feast of St. John the Baptist). This is considered the beginning of the apparitions of Our Lady to six young people on Podbrdo hill in Medjugorje.

June 25th: Day of the Queen of Peace. Anniversary of the apparitions. On this day, the six men spoke with Our Lady for the first time.

July 25: Day of St. James: The parish of Medjugorje is named after St. James (feast day in Medjugorje).

August 5: Our Lady's Birthday - (According to Revelation)

March 25, 1985: Announcement of the tenth secret to the visionary Vicka Ivanković-Mijatović.

January 25, 1987: Apparition of Our Lady on the hill of Podbrdo after a period of silence.

November 11, 1987: A little daughter is born in Ivanka's house. Her name: Christina.

August 15, 1988: Our Lady calls for a year of youth.

August 15, 1989: At the request of the Blessed Mother, another year is dedicated to the youth and also a year for the family.

August 25, 1991: Our Lady announces the tenth secret to the visionary Ivanka Ivanković-Mijatović.

December 25, 1992: Last daily apparition of Our Lady to Ivanka Ivanković-Mijatović.

June 25, 2007: Monthly apparition of Our Lady to Ivanka Ivanković-Mijatović continues, revealing only one annual message.

December 25, 2017: Ivanka Ivanković-Mijatović reveals that Our Lady has entrusted her with the ninth and tenth mysteries, but does not specify their content.

June 25, 2021: Celebration of the 40th anniversary of the apparitions with the presence of several visionaries and pilgrims.

2.2 "MARY, QUEEN OF PEACE", THIS IS HOW OUR LADY PRESENTS HERSELF IN MEDJUGORJE

The apparitions of Medjugorje, which began on June 24, 1981, have had an impact on Bosnia-Herzegovina (formerly Yugoslavia, but divided into several territories in 1992). The situation is similar to that of Lourdes in 1958. The number of articles and publications on this subject has multiplied, and today Medjugorje can no longer be ignored. Our Lady invites us to believe without delay, because tomorrow it could be too late. The six visionaries at the beginning of the apparitions were between 11 and 17 years old, with significant differences in personality, age and intellectual capacity. Before the apparitions, they did not stand out among the other children of the parish for their devotion, nor for their participation in catechism or the sacraments. They are not religious fanatics; they are simple and friendly, in short, they are normal children. It is important to remember that an apparition is not a reward for merit or effort, but a free gift given for the good of the community.

2.3 THE FIRST APPARITIONS - (A STORY BY FR. JOZO - AUGUST 1988)

On June 24, 1981, some boys went up Podbrdo Mountain looking for some sheep, but they did not find them. Instead, they found a great light blocking their way. After the light appeared the figure of the Virgin Mary. They were out of breath and could not speak, they could only look. When they saw the Virgin again, they were filled with fear and ran. It was not until they reached the courtyard of their homes that they were able to breathe. Six of them saw both the light and the Virgin, while nine saw only the light. Nevertheless, they all believed immediately.

The original visionaries of the apparitions of Our Lady in Medjugorje are six young people who all saw Our Lady on Podbrdo. The names of the visionaries are

a) Ivan Dragičević: Born on May 25, 1965. He has a night prayer group where sometimes the Virgin Mary gives him messages. He is married with three children and lives between the United States and Medjugorje. His main prayer request is to pray for young people and priests.

b) Mirjana Dragičević: Born on March 18, 1965. Every second day of the month, Our Lady sends her public messages to those who do not believe. She lives in Medugorje, is married and has two daughters. Our Lady asked her to pray especially for those who do not yet have faith.

c) Vicka Ivanković: Born on September 3, 1964. Our Lady told her about her life for three years and she wrote it down in three notebooks that only she can read. She is married, has a daughter and lives in Krehin Grac, near Medjugorje. Although she has suffered from various illnesses, her main prayer wish is to pray for the health of the sick.

d) Marija Pavlović: Born on April 1, 1965. Every 25th day she receives a public message from the Virgin Mary. She is married, has four children and divides her time between Italy and Medjugorje. Our Lady asked her to pray especially for the souls in purgatory.

e) Ivanka Ivanković: Born on June 21, 1966. She was the first person to see Our Lady, and the last time she saw Our Lady on a daily basis, she saw her deceased mother next to Our Lady. She is married, has three children and lives in Medjugorje. Her main intention is to pray for families.

f) Jakov Colo: Born on March 6, 1971. Together with the visionary Vicka, they were physically taken to heaven, purgatory and hell. He is married, has three children and lives in Medjugorje. His main prayer intention is to pray for the health of the sick.

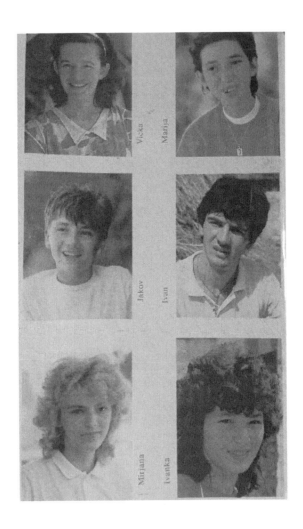

Vicka

Marija

Jakov

Ivan

Mirjana

Ivanka

Ivanka Ivankovic.   Jakov Colo.   Ivan Dragicevic.

Vicka Ivankovic.   Marija Pavlovic.   Mirjana Dragicevic.

2.4 VICKA'S GRANDMOTHER'S OPINION

The parents were worried about their children, thinking that the intense heat might affect them mentally. All night long they discussed the situation and no one believed in the apparitions except the children, who kept their faith and waited anxiously for the next day to see the Virgin.

It was not easy for the visionaries to propose the idea of going to the mountain together, because the people judged them relentlessly for claiming that the Virgin had appeared to them, considering it a sin. Despite the criticism, the children remained steadfast, insisting that they were only sharing what they had seen. However, people wanted them to give up this belief.

Vicka's grandmother intervened and expressed her doubts: "How can you be sure that it is Our Lady? Even Satan can appear. If they haven't prayed, how can they say it's Our Lady? When a Christian prays, Satan goes away".

After much discussion, everyone decided to go to the mountain. Like the day before, a light appeared from the left side and everyone in the parish knelt on the thorns unharmed. Following her grandmother's advice, Vicka began to pray with a flower dipped in holy water, making the sign of the cross and saying, "If you are Satan, go far away. Our Lady smiled and said, "Do not be afraid.

2.5 I HAVE CHOSEN THEM, I HAVE CALLED THEM

After reciting the Creed, Vicka said, "Did you notice anything? We did not lie. We told the truth; you saw and heard." But the others only saw a light and did not have the same experience. Although there were signs for everyone, it was difficult to believe. My parents and I were skeptical, thinking that the young people might be under the influence of drugs. But the faithful in the parish trusted and stayed awake in Podbrdo because they saw the sign in the open heart.

Our Lady had told them: "I have chosen you, I have called you".

These four words are very important and affected the visionaries very much. In every situation they know that "Our Lady needs them". They feel responsible and are ready to do whatever Our Lady asks of them. Although they were persecuted, they never denied the truth, even when it would have been easier. The police followed them, even to their home.

One day Jakov said, "Tomorrow Our Lady will appear in the church. I asked him, "Yesterday you said it was in Podbrdo, and before that in the vineyards. I asked him, "Yesterday you said it was on Podbrdo, before that among the vineyards, and now you say it will be in the church tomorrow. How can I believe you?" Jakov replied, "I cannot help you because you do not believe. I thought, "How can I believe you? Who are you that I should believe?" St. Luke wrote in his Gospel (Chapter IV) that Jesus could not perform miracles in his own town because of lack of faith. He went to another nearby town, Cana of Galilee, where he performed a beautiful miracle at a wedding. But he could not help the people in his own town because they did not believe.

2.6 THE PRIEST WHO BEGINS TO BELIEVE

When I turned on the microphone, I thought, 'My parish is going through a difficult situation. We need to pray, because there is only curiosity here. We were in the church from noon and I celebrated Mass at 6. After Mass, Jakov announced that Our Lady was asking us to pray the rosary. Everyone wanted to stay and pray together. During the rosary, Our Lady appeared and repeated the same words that Jakov had said after Mass. That night I began to believe. I became a believer, but not when I heard Our Lady's voice, as someone said, but when I opened my heart. Only then did I hear Our Lady's voice repeating the same words that Jakov had said.

2.7 MIRJANA DRAGICEVIC

She was the first to stop seeing the Blessed Mother daily. By Christmas of 1982, she had received her tenth apparition. At present, Our Lady appears to her on her birthday and on special occasions. She got married in September 1989. Mirjana tells us: The person who believes in God and opens her heart to Him should not be afraid. God will always be with her...

2.8 IVANKA IVANKOVIC

She also no longer sees Our Lady every day. On May 6, 1985, Our Lady revealed to her the tenth secret and promised to see her every year on the anniversary of the apparitions. Ivanka got married in December 1986. Ivanka tells us Return to God as soon as possible, because He is the only one who will lead you to happiness and truth. For this we must pray a lot and live the messages of Medjugorje.

2.9 IVAN DRAGICEVIC

In June 1987, he completed his year of military service. He continues to have daily apparitions in the Church. Our Lady has shown me my future. I trust and I am not afraid, because I know who is guiding me and therefore I am not afraid of death. All people should feel this way.

2.10   MARIJA PAVLOVIC

After the apparitions, she will join a religious order. I always tell people that they should pray more and that the Lord will give them the peace they need in everything that burdens them. If people accept the messages, God will guide them.

2.11   JACOV COLO

He is the youngest. The Blessed Mother has begun to explain to him the future of the Church and the world. He currently works in the parish bookstore. Since I saw Our Lady, my life has changed completely. Now I pray more and go to Mass every night. I feel closer to God. For me, Mass is an encounter with the living God. Our Mother always tells us to pray more.

2.12   VICKA IVANKOVIC

For two years he had the revelation of the life of the Blessed Mother, that is, the Virgin Mary revealed to him what her life was like. "I feel sad for those who still do not believe in God. Great things are happening here: the Mother of God is among us. She wants to lead everyone to her Son. That is why she has come for so long and so often. Here everyone feels the closeness and the love of God".

2.13   THE SECRETS

The seers keep most of the details of the ten special messages they received, known as the Ten Secrets, secret. The last two messages speak of punishments for the world's mistakes. The seers know when these secrets will be revealed and claim that three days later there will be a sign on the mountain for those who do not believe, a sign that will remain. No other details are known. The Virgin Mary has said that the best sign is always Christian behavior. On one occasion she said: "You, the believers, have received many signs to believe, and now you yourselves must be signs for those who do not believe. In this time of waiting for signs, it is essential not to waste time in curiosity and speculation, but to use it for prayer and conversion. "This is the time of grace. When the sign comes, it may be too late for many to convert," Our Lady warned.

2.14   MESSAGES

According to the testimony of the six visionaries, in each apparition Our Lady told them the various messages she had to give to humanity. These messages were numerous, but the fundamental ones can be summarized in five.

2.15   THE PEACE

From the third day on, Our Lady gave a decisive message: PEACE, PEACE, PEACE - ONLY PEACE - RECONCILE WITH ONE ANOTHER. IF THE WORLD WANTS TO BE SAVED, IT MUST SEEK THE WAY OF PEACE. Peace comes through conversion, prayer and fasting. The world will find peace only when it returns to God. On August 6, 1981, at 6:15 p.m., the word MIR, which means PEACE, appeared in luminous letters in the sky of Medjugorje. Our Lady emphasizes the importance of finding inner peace before sharing it with others. She encourages us to put God's peace in our hearts and to live it first and then to spread it. Our Lady warns that turning away from God leads to loss of peace and hatred. Her desire is to bring peace to Medjugorje and for the Pope to bring it to the world. According to Our Lady, peace comes through prayer and only Jesus Christ can bring spiritual peace when we meet Him.

2.16   PRAYER PEACE

Mary, Mother of God, my Mother, Queen of Peace, ask your Son Jesus to give me the gift of peace. Pray that I may have peace: peace in my heart, peace of mind and soul, peace in my family, peace with all those I meet on my way, the peace of Jesus. Jesus, my Lord and Savior, my brother, the King of Peace, I come to you with Mary, the Queen of Peace, to humbly ask you for the gift of peace. Pour out on me Your Holy Spirit of Peace. Give me peace, Jesus, peace in me, peace in my family, peace in every day of my life. Give my country and every nation peace. Peace for all, peace in the world. Jesus, my intercessor with the Father, take me to the Father to pray for peace. Father, Father of Jesus, our Father, my Father, I come to You with Your Son Jesus. In Him, with Him and through Him I pray for peace.

(Fr. Herbert Faricy's prayer for Christmas 1984).

CHAPTER 3: PRAYER AND ITS MEANING IN MEDJUGORJE

In this third chapter, I would like to present to you the importance of prayer and its great relevance in

Medjugorje. It is very important that we strengthen our faith so that we can believe in the goodness that Our Lady wants to transmit to us. If we do not have faith, we will not be able to feel the love of God in our hearts. One day I heard someone's words from heaven that made me feel loved and gave me the courage to go on with my life. This last thing I just wrote is a demonstration of faith, it is believing in the inexplicable, believing in the things that sometimes children believe and that we think are just imagination. If you can have faith, then your connection with the spiritual will be pure and clear, and that is the way to feel God, Jesus, the Virgin Mary, and even the connection with your loved ones who have left this world, as we saw in the previous chapter with Ivanka's experience of seeing her deceased mother with the Virgin Mary. This chapter may seem boring because of the topics I am dealing with, but you should thoroughly analyze each point and determine how you can improve.

3.1 IN MEDJUGORJE, A STATE OF INTENSE PRAYER IS EXPERIENCED IN MEDJUGORJE - SPIRITUAL ENERGY MEASURED SCIENTIFICALLY

Dr. Lipinski, Director of the Boston Cardiovascular Center and President of the International Association for Electricity Studies, conducted a study in Medjugorje using a device called the BT Electroscope to measure the energy during the apparitions. The unit of measurement is one millradius per hour. For comparison, the tolerable dose in Hiroshima is 0.1 millrads per day.

The readings on March 15, 1985, were surprisingly high, reaching one million millrads per hour. Dr. Lipinski initially thought that there might be radioactive substances at the site of the apparitions that could affect the visionaries, but found no evidence of this. His conclusions indicate that the cause of these phenomena is "truly supernatural. He also points out that the increased energy is not due to the number of people present, but to the quality of the people present.

The study also revealed that the day with the highest reading coincided with a fasting Friday, suggesting that fasting may have a particular effect on the value of the reading and that the energy observed is spiritual in nature.

3.2 FAITH

The Virgin Mary encourages us to have faith because she considers it essential to our prayers and aspirations. Her main message is that God exists and represents the fullness of life. She also encourages us to love all people, regardless of their religion. While recognizing her Son, Jesus Christ, as the only Mediator and Savior, Our Lady emphasizes the importance of living according to our conscience and taking our religion seriously.

According to Our Lady, conversion involves changing our attitudes, thoughts and feelings. She urges us to put away what separates us from God, to purify our hearts, and to confess our sins. To facilitate this conversion, she provides us with means such as prayer, the rosary, reading the Bible, attending Mass and fasting.

Our Lady stresses the importance of making changes before it is too late and urges us to be a living example of faith to others. She reminds us that there is strength in prayer. Living according to her message means accepting what God offers us and rejecting what evil offers us.

Our Lady urges us to seek first the Kingdom of God and to concentrate on prayer and conversion. She recommends fasting and devoting daily time to prayer in order to achieve radical change and obtain the peace that Jesus Christ, the Prince of Peace, offers us.

3.3 PRAYER, FASTING AND THE ROSARY

Fasting helps us to be in control of ourselves, and only those who are in control of themselves can be truly free and give themselves to God and to others, as faith demands. The Virgin Mary does not ask us to go hungry, but to live a life of simplicity and humility, with our hearts open to the Lord. She suggests fasting on bread and water, especially on Fridays, and emphasizes that the sick are exempt.

Peace, healing and every grace for body and soul are inaccessible without prayer and fasting. Our Lady suggests that fasting can even prevent wars and urges us to pray and fast together to achieve everything. With regard to prayer, she points out that many families disintegrate for lack of this habit and encourages us to find time for spontaneous dialog with God. Prayer is essential to live with God and to find inner peace.

Our Lady invites us to prayer of the heart and advises us to thank God for everything. She also exhorts us to love our neighbor and to offer our hearts to be transformed. She encourages us to pray the Rosary daily and to attend Mass, emphasizing that the Rosary is not just an ornament, but should be a contemplative prayer. He also stresses the importance of the Mass as the most sublime form of prayer.

As for the prophecies and revelations, the Virgin Mary presents them as a call to faith and conversion. She does not promise an easy future, because she knows that we all carry our own burdens on earth. Her apparition in Medjugorje is a simple and consistent reminder of truths forgotten by the world, offering love and service to God in today's humanity.

3.4 MORE ABOUT FASTING

The Scriptures mention fasting, a practice that has been lost in the Church today. The word "fast" comes from expressions meaning "to cover one's mouth" or "not to eat. It is a voluntary abstinence from food, not as an end in itself, but as a way to holiness. Our Lady in Medjugorje pointed out that we have forgotten its meaning and suggested that the best form is the fast of bread and water, although there are other ways to practice it.

In Medjugorje, the emphasis is on the fast of bread and water, which has a deep meaning. The bread represents the food of the poor. The call to fast is a repetition of what Jesus and the early Church practiced. Through prayer we connect with God, and through fasting we free our hearts from earthly bonds. This new freedom allows us to adopt new values and improves the quality of our prayer.

We need fasting to grow in prayer, especially in prayer of the heart. Prayer becomes easier when we fast, and fasting is more effective when we pray. Fasting frees us from certain bondage and allows us to experience joy, an inner peace that helps us overcome difficult situations. Through fasting, our heart becomes pure and we perceive reality more clearly.

Fasting helps us to discriminate what is essential in life and reminds us that we are pilgrims in this world. Many people would be happy with a roof over their heads and a little bread, but often we are not satisfied even though we have plenty. Fasting helps us to see what is essential and leads us to search for God with Mary. Being a pilgrim means developing a new daily relationship, opening our hearts to those in need and recognizing the spiritual and material needs of others.

Fasting with the heart means loving and accepting our journey with God and Mary, choosing freedom over slavery to material things. It also means to deepen our joy in the Lord. Fasting and prayer are means to guide us in the search for peace, to be the prayer of the whole body and to demonstrate that our body should participate fully in prayer.

3.5 PRAYER ON FASTING DAYS

O Lord God, my Creator, today I thank you for this beautiful world that you have made. Thank you for the food that comes from the earth. Today I have decided to fast to hear more of your word and to grow closer to you. I offer this fast for peace in the world and for those who are too focused on the material.

I repent for any misuse of material goods in the past. Through this fast I want my love for You and for my fellow man to grow in me. May I better understand the value of the heavenly bread, the presence of Your Son in the Eucharist, and may my faith and trust in You grow.

Father, I ask you to help me understand the needs of the hungry and thirsty and to see what I possess but do not need. Give my heart humility and a stronger desire to do your will. Cleanse me of selfishness and pride, and through this fast, free me from bad habits as your virtues grow in me.

May my soul be open to your grace and may I resist every temptation to serve you and seek your word every day. Mary, pray for me that I may do this fast with joy and perseverance. I offer the hardship and hunger I will feel today for the whole world.

Mary, teach me to fast and to pray so that day by day I may become more like You and Your Son, Jesus Christ, in the Holy Spirit. Amen.

3.6 MORE ABOUT PRAYER

We know that Jesus tells us to pray always, without ceasing. However, many times we find excuses and say that we don't have time to pray. But the problem is not only whether we have time, but whether we really feel the need to know God through prayer. As we desire more things and accumulate more, we sometimes leave less space and time for God. We settle for having more material things and think that this will solve all our problems. But prayer is like food for our soul, something we need every day. If we ask God with faith and perseverance, the gift of prayer will be born in our hearts.

3.7 WORDS OF FR. TOMISLAV VLASIC ABOUT PRAYER

We need to discover how valuable it is to pray, and these messages help us to develop and deepen this practice. Prayer involves a personal transformation that positively affects our lives. Sometimes some people pray like those who are outside the church, asking for earthly benefits such as health and happiness without fully surrendering themselves to God. On the other hand, those who truly surrender to God experience the fullness of His graces by focusing only on the divine.

Weeping, fighting, and suffering for God are actions that come from being in the heart of God. Sometimes our prayers are not heard because we are not willing to give ourselves completely to the Lord. Those who live for God are those who truly possess Him. The amount of our prayer brings us to the minimum or maximum of our Christian life.

Prayer is nourished by the Bible, and it is important to read it with the heart, not just with the eyes. Just as we devote time to television, magazines, or conversation, we must devote time to reading the Bible. When the Bible takes root in our hearts, we think and form ourselves as children of God, which enables us to pray. The Bible contains the living Word of the Lord, anointed by the Holy Spirit. Reading the Bible is not just observing words on paper, but connecting with the Lord who lives and speaks through it.

3.8 HOW TO PRAY - PRIEST TOMISLAV VLASIC

Fr. Tomislav Vlasic presents a prayer itinerary for finding God in everyday life.

a) HAVING GOD AS THE FIRST VALUE

Many people pray, but they do not seek God. To seek God is to desire what God wants, to realize what He wants. Seeking God means first of all to devote some time to prayer. We have to sacrifice many things to get the opportunity to pray. You learn to pray by praying. We cannot have peace if we do not put God in the center of our lives. Not relying on God, not praising Him, not thanking Him, is like putting God in a corner. We cannot be satisfied with a few minutes of prayer in the morning or going to confession once a year. How could the Lord Jesus pray all night long without getting tired? By what method? He had a great desire for God and a great desire to save souls. The fundamental commandment of Christianity is to be in love with God, to love God with all our strength, and to love our neighbor as ourselves. God is found in prayer.

b) DEDICATE SOME TIME TO GOD

If we love God, we must devote our time exclusively to Him. Just as we say: "At such and such an hour we eat," we should say: *At such and such an hour one prays. Sometimes we pray in haste, as if we were ringing a bell and pretending to get everything done quickly. No, prayer, like all important things, takes a long time. It is a mistake to say: "This can only be said by those who pray a lot during the day. At the beginning of the apparitions, Our Lady asked us to pray the seven Our Fathers, the seven Hail Marys and the seven Glorias (one for the gift of the Holy Spirit, one for the Holy Father and five for the sacred wounds of Jesus Christ for the conversion of sinners), because Christians who do not pray are not believers. Also a creed for those who do not believe.

c) CREATE A SPACE FOR GOD IN THE HOUSE

Let us put God instead of the television and the television in a corner. It is also important for the education of the children and for all of you to have an atmosphere of recollection in which there is the visible presence of God: a crucifix, a statue, a picture in front of which you gather to pray.

d) ENTER INTO PRAYER WITH PEACE

Our prayer should be born of peace and lead us to peace. When you enter into prayer, do so with your body at rest; sit or kneel down calmly. Put yourselves in a state of humility before God, like children in their mother's arms. Lean on God, tell Him your worries, talk to Him about everything that is happening to you. To create this spiritual climate of peace, read a short passage from the Gospel. Read it twice and, with your eyes closed, let it sink deep into your heart. The way of prayer is designed to lead us to a personal encounter with God, in Jesus Christ, through the Holy Spirit.

e) TRANSLATING PRAYER INTO LIFE

"If you want to be stronger against evil," Our Lady said on Good Friday, 1984, "make yourselves an active conscience, that is, pray enough in the morning, read a part of the Gospel and engrave the Word of God in your hearts, and then live it during the day, especially in trials. Our prayers should not remain in a closed circle: praying for the sake of praying, without any transformation. Let us start by getting rid of so many useless things in our homes so that God can be in the first place. You will be freer and happier. Our Lady, in her earthly life, was contemplative, but now in heaven, as the Second Vatican Council says, she is "active" because "with her maternal love she takes care of the brothers and sisters of her Son who are still on pilgrimage and in danger, until they are led to the homeland of beatitude" (LG 62).

3.9 SPIRITUAL FRUITS

Medjugorje is becoming more and more known as a place where people are profoundly changed. It is unique among pilgrimage sites in the world, with millions of visitors from all over the world and from different religions (more than those who have visited Lourdes so far). Although it attracts mainly Catholics, it also attracts non-Christians. Some of them, even without being baptized, have come to Medjugorje and have asked for and received baptism before returning home. A beautiful and encouraging aspect of Medjugorje is that there are vocations to religious and priestly life.

The Archbishop of Split, Moseignor Frane Franic, stated that "never, nowhere, not even in Lourdes or Fatima, has there been greater religiosity".

In Medjugorje, people begin to see things from a faith perspective. The most important thing that people are looking for is not physical miracles, but a better understanding of sickness and other sufferings from the perspective of faith. In the faces of the pilgrims you can see the happiness that comes from repentance, conversion and purification. People seek deep healing of the heart, mind and spiritual blindness. They ask for conversion, light and strength to carry the cross and follow Christ. Even those who did not know how to pray before now know how to pray. Those who were slaves to sin now feel liberated.

In these difficult times for the Church and her growth in faith, the Virgin Mary tries to help her children with extraordinary interventions to draw them closer to God and to grow in faith. Millions of pilgrims, conversions, stronger faith, deeper prayer, confessions and communions, sincere devotion and a new Christian spirit in the pilgrims are obvious fruits of Our Lady's apparitions and actions in Medjugorje. They are also an announcement of the victory over evil.

The deep reason for Our Lady's apparitions, messages and long stay in Medjugorje is her motherly love for all people, especially in these difficult and dangerous times. Her motherly love does not allow her to be visibly separated from her children until she assures their salvation. This is the reason why Our Lady appeared, why She gave messages and why Her apparitions are so long.

3.10 OTHER IMPORTANT MESSAGES THE HOLY VIRGIN HAS GIVEN US ABOUT THE HOLY MASS

"Mass is the best and most complete prayer. I urge you to attend Mass, if possible, every day. Prepare yourself and participate more with your heart. Many people go to Mass without preparation and without approaching Communion, so Mass is worth very little. The best time to ask for graces is at the moment of consecration. One cannot thank God enough for the immense gift of the Eucharist. My children, I hope that Holy Mass will be the gift of the day for you. Wait for it, hope that it will come soon. Jesus gives himself. During Mass, long for that moment when you will be purified. I am closer to you during Mass than during the apparitions

3.11   ABOUT LOVE

Our Lady, with her countless apparitions, her wise counsels and her extraordinary catechesis, has made Medjugorje a true school of holiness, where the greatest and most important lesson is that of love. **"Dear children, today I invite you to live this week the words: I love God! With love you will achieve everything; even those things that seem impossible to you, live love for God and for your brothers and sisters. I want to engrave the seal of love in every heart. If you love all people, there will be peace in you. I love you and if you want to understand My love, you must start to love, ask God to give you all the gifts of love that you are lacking. I am the Teacher and I have come to teach you the program; to pray with love. I invite you to love your family first and then you will be able to accept everyone else."**

At midnight on August 4, 1987, the Croatian word Ljubav, which means LOVE, appeared as if written in the clouds in the serene sky of Mount Podbrdo (where the first apparitions took place). The inscription shone for about 10 minutes in the presence of about 10,000 pilgrims from all over the world who came to celebrate the anniversary of Our Lady's birth. (In the course of 1984, Our Lady confided to the visionaries that the date of her birth was August 5).

"Love your enemies, implore God's blessing upon them. I know that you are not able to love your enemies. **That is why you should pray for five minutes every day. To my heart and to the heart of my Son, and we will give you the divine love with which you will be able to love everyone.** I thank you for all the sacrifices you have offered, offer them with love. I love you, dear children, with a special love and I want to take you all to heaven with God. I want you to understand that this life is short compared to heaven. God does not want you to be lukewarm and indecisive, but to give yourselves completely to Him. You know that I love you and burn with love for you. Therefore, make up your minds to live love and know the love of God day by day.

"Children, what else can I tell you but to have a little love for others; even in this Satan hinders you. Love for others is when you can be together for something, when you can sing, when you can talk, when you can shake someone's hand with your heart... when you greet them with your heart, when you speak and do not wish them ill, when you do not say to another person: "You are like that. When you want to tell this person how beautiful she is, when you explain the truths and you feel good about it because these words are dictated by God, when you tell her that you want to help her. To love another person, you must love everything in him: this means loving Jesus in that person; Jesus is loved in prayer, but also with his works. Dear children, if someone does not want to talk to you, act as if it were not so. Be silent, do not make your way heard, that is, do not comment to others that this person is like this. Just let it remain in your heart that you love that person all the time".

3.12   ON THE BLESSED SACRAMENT

Regarding adoration of the Blessed Sacrament, Our Lady said to the visionaries one day: "Today I am especially grateful to you because you have come to adore the Blessed Sacrament. I am always present when the faithful are in adoration.

"Special graces are received at that time. **Visit the Blessed Sacrament at least once a week."**

3.13   ABOUT PRAYER

"You have forgotten that by prayer and fasting you can avert wars, and if they have begun, you can make them cease. You can even suspend the laws of nature, that is, work miracles. Many Christians have lost their faith because they do not pray. Prayer is the way to peace. When you pray, a fountain of life will gush forth from your hearts. Let prayer rule your hearts every moment. In it you will find the deepest joy".

"Through the priests, I want to lead the people deep into prayer. Place the Bible in the center of your home, in a visible place, so that the desire to read it and pray with it will come to you. Always pray before you begin your daily activities. And even when you have finished your work, return to prayer; if you do, God will bless you and your work. Pray more for the conversion of sinners. Without your prayers there can be no peace. Recite the rosary as a family. Renew prayer in your families. Encourage the little ones to pray and let the children come to Holy Mass. I thank all of you who have increased prayer in your families. Pray to the Holy Spirit to enlighten you. Ask for the gift of the Holy Spirit; if you have this gift, you will lack nothing. Pray with your heart and not by rote, turn your hearts to prayer and strive for the Holy Spirit to be poured out on you!

Let prayer be your daily food. Pray and you will be able to overcome any weariness. Let prayer be your joy and your rest. Prayer must be sealed with peace: at the beginning, in its development and at the end. Inner listening is necessary. Pray a complete Rosary every day. The Rosary is not a decoration for the house. It is to be prayed. Dear children, put on the armor against Satan and defeat him with the Rosary in your hands. Pray it with living faith and great recollection. Without prayer you will not be able to feel God, nor me, nor the grace I am giving you. Always give first place to prayer. I invite you to make your prayer a joyful encounter with the Lord. When you pray, you are much more beautiful, like the flowers that after the snow show all their beauty and their colors become indescribable. In the same way, dear children, after you pray, you show even more before God all the beauty for which God is pleased with you. Pray without ceasing and live all the messages I am giving you. God gives special graces in prayer. Pray that God's blessing may protect you from all the evil that threatens you. May prayer be life for you! Dedicate your time only to Jesus and He will give you everything you are looking for. He will reveal Himself to you in fullness. Dear children, Satan is strong and is waiting to test each one of you. Pray! Then he will not be able to harm you or hinder you on the path of holiness. Grow more and more in prayer every day."

3.14   WHAT IS THE PRAYER OF THE HEART?

Fr. Tomislav Vlasic answers: When a person goes on the path of prayer with his heart, then God becomes everything. The person is filled with God. This union between man and God does not take place on the level of emotionality. Depending on how one progresses in the prayer of the heart, the following virtues become more and more manifest: peace, silence, joy-which is born of deep peace and silence-humility, understanding, and love. God's joy is not like human joy. Many celebrations of young people end in tiredness, but whoever enters into prayer of the heart enters into a celebration that does not tire, the strength increases more and more. and "Sorrow looks back, sorrow looks forward, faith looks upward.

The future belongs to the Lord. He has a sign of "no passage"; if you pass through, the punishment you receive is sorrow. We carry on our shoulders many worries about tomorrow and we are unable to face today because we are tired of yesterday and afraid of tomorrow. The Blessed Virgin Mary really wants us to live the present, and that is why she asked the Medjugorje prayer groups to meditate on the following text every Thursday during adoration of the Blessed Sacrament:

MATTHEW 6:24-34. "No one can serve two masters, for either he will hate the one and love the other, or he will be devoted to the one and despise the other. You cannot serve God and money. So I tell you, do not worry about your life, what you will eat, or about your body, what you will wear. Is not life more important than food, and the body more important than clothing? Look at the birds of the air; they neither sow nor reap, nor gather into barns; and your heavenly Father feeds them. Are you not more valuable than they? For which of you, no matter how much he cares, can add a cubit to the measure of his life? and why do you care about clothing? Behold the lilies of the field, how they grow; they do not toil, nor do they spin. But I tell you, not even Solomon in all his glory was clothed like one of them. For if the grass of the field, which is today and tomorrow is cast into the oven, is thus clothed by God, will he not much more clothe you, O ye of little faith? Therefore do not be anxious, saying, "What shall we eat, what shall we drink, what shall we wear? For the Gentiles are anxious about all these things; for your heavenly Father knows that you have need of all these things. But seek first his kingdom and his righteousness, and all these things will be given to you as well. so do not worry about tomorrow; tomorrow will take care of itself. Each day has its own evil.

3.15   ON CONFESSION

On August 2, 1981, the visionaries had a little known experience. Fr. Tomislav tells us that while the visionaries were praying in the woods with about fifty people, Our Lady appeared to them. At the end of the apparition, they saw the visionary weeping; she was crying because they had soiled Our Lady's dress. Our Lady explained: "THOSE WHO LIVE IN SIN HAVE SOILED HER, TELL THE

PEOPLE TO COME TO CONFESS AND MAKE REPARATION FOR THEIR SINS".

3.16   IN CONNECTION WITH THE CONFESSION THE VIRGIN SAID:

"If Christians would begin to reconcile with God and people once a month, they would soon be spiritually healed. They should not go to confession as a matter of routine and then remain the same. Confession should give a new impulse to their faith, it should shake them up and bring them closer to God". If confession does not mean something important to you, you will hardly be converted. The visionaries affirm that before going to the Sacrament of Penance, one should prepare oneself not for five minutes, but for the whole day.

3.17   HOW TO PRAY FOR THE SICK

Our Lady says: "I cannot heal you, only God can. Turn to Jesus because I am your Mother and I will intercede for you before Him, but let every prayer be addressed to Jesus. It is God who will heal you. I am not God. I will help you, I will pray for you, but not everything depends on me. The power of those who pray is also necessary. I need you to help me with your prayers and your sacrifices to get these healings. Come to me if you want me to intercede for you. I know what God's will is. The most important thing is to have faith. If there are serious illnesses, fast twice a week. If possible, get some of you together to pray for the sick. In praying for the sick, Our Lady also recommended perseverance: "Many sick people come to church, begin to pray and soon stop. This is not good".

During the apparition of June 22, 1985, Jelena Vasilj says that Our Lady gave her a special prayer to pray for the sick: "Dear children, this is the most beautiful prayer that can be prayed for a sick person. Jesus wants that when this prayer is prayed, both the sick person and the person praying for him/her place themselves completely in the hands of God.

Oh my God!

this sick man who is here before YOU,

has come to ask You what he wants and what he thinks and what is most important to him.

You, O God,

let these words enter his heart

"It is more important to be healed in the soul!"

Lord, be upon him

Your holy will in all things.

If you want him to be healed

that he be given health.

But if Your will is otherwise,

that he continue to carry his cross.

We also pray for us

that we may pray for him;

purify our hearts

that we may be worthy to give,

by ourselves,

Your holy mercy.

Protect him and alleviate his sorrows,

May your holy will be done in him.

May Your holy name be manifested through him,

Help him to bear his cross with love.

Amen.

CHAPTER 4: THE IMPRESSIVE AND EXTRAORDINARY OF MEDJUGORJE

Thank you for having reached this chapter, from now on I am going to present to you some events, dates, testimonies and some other information that are absolutely unbelievable and extraordinary. In order to experience them as I really want you to experience them, I would like to ask you to imagine that you are in Medjugorje, a small town cut off from the world, and to imagine all the facts and events that will be narrated below. This will give you a very deep experience of faith, love for yourself, love for others and true love for God and the Blessed Virgin Mary.

4.1 THE SYMBOLIC MESSAGE OF THE NAMES

Draga Ivankovic, who lives in Medjugorje, revealed that one of the visionaries discovered the deep meaning of their names:

Mirjana and Maria means MARY

Ivanka and Iván means JUAN

Jakov means SANTIAGO

Vicka means LIFE

MEANING: MARY appeared in the PARISH OF THE APOSTOL OF SANTIAGO OF MEDIUGORJE on the feast of ST. JOHN THE BAPTIST to bring LIFE.

4.2 TO JESUS FOR MARY

Throughout these years of apparitions, we realize that the Blessed Virgin does not announce herself in the messages. On the contrary, she seeks the glory of the Father and of Jesus Christ. "I am a good mother and Jesus is your great friend. Do not be afraid to be in His company, but give Him your heart. Tell him your sufferings from the depths of your free heart, in fearless peace. Let us remember the testimony of David Duplessis, who, on his way to Medjugorje, waited everywhere for the name of Mary and was surprised: **"The name that is most often proclaimed is that of Jesus."**

4.3 FOR THOSE WHO ARE DEPRESSED OR DISCOURAGED

One day Our Lady said something very beautiful. Satan often takes advantage of a person who feels unworthy of God, who feels very depressed and discouraged: this is the moment when the enemy, very cowardly, takes advantage of this to take him away from God. Our Lady told us to fix this idea in our minds: "**God is your Father and He does not care how you are. Do not let Satan influence you, not even for a moment, because he is very strong. For example, if you have committed a sin, if you have quarreled with someone, don't stay alone, call God immediately, ask for forgiveness, and go on**". After committing a sin, we start to think and doubt whether God can forgive us. This is not so. We always measure God by our guilt. We think, If the sin is small, God will forgive me immediately; if the sin is serious, He will take more time. For you it takes more time to recognize your sins, but not for God, the Lord forgives immediately, and you must be ready to ask and receive His forgiveness, without leaving time for the enemy to take advantage of these moments of dissolution and desertion.

4.4 VISIONARY VICKA SHARES HER VISION OF HEAVEN, PURGATORY AND HELL

"Paradise is something wonderful and indescribable, everything is filled with a wonderful light, people, flowers, angels. Everything is filled with unspeakable joy. In a word, it is so beautiful that your heart stops when you look at it.

"Purgatory is a dark, gloomy place, between paradise and hell, full of ashes. It looks terrible. It is the place where souls are purified, and Our Lady has told us that it is necessary to pray a lot for them."

"From hell I saw fire, demons, terrible people, they suffer a lot. They blaspheme against God. I saw people before they went in, when they fell, and then when they came out. They came out transformed into beasts. Those who fall there can never be saved.

Our Lady explained to the visionaries that none of those who are in Purgatory or Hell are being punished by God, "God does not condemn or punish anyone," Our Lady told them, "Those who are there are there because they want to be there. They have chosen that place themselves. "God gives each person the freedom to decide where he will go when he dies.

Man, blinded by the attraction of material goods and the realities that surround him, becomes so attached that he often and easily forgets the realities that await him in the next life. That is why Our Lady, like a good mother, comes to remind us of these truths, showing them clearly to the visionaries and through them to us in Paradise, Purgatory and Hell, using images that the eye and mind of man can understand.

To Mirian in particular, He revealed things that neither she nor we understand clearly enough, such as the contrast between infinite mercy and the eternity of hell. She explained that the eternity of hell is based on the hatred the damned have for God, which is why they do not even want to leave hell.

4.5 OUR LADY'S MESSAGE TO BROTHER DAVID

"Tell the people, my children, that the 8th and the 12th of December are special days, in a special way, for those groups who will gather at noon to pray the 15 mysteries of the Rosary and after each 5 mysteries pray Psalm 50, mainly to ask God for my petition, which is the outpouring of the Holy Spirit on the whole Church, so that the Church will be a catalyst for the renewal of the world; and for those who cannot go to a group because of commitments, to bring their petitions to any group that will join this prayer. I have received from my Son Jesus that all the requests made during these days will be granted". December 8 and 12, the feasts of the Immaculate Conception and Our Lady of Guadalupe, are "special" in that, according to the liturgy, special graces are associated with the great feasts.

4.6 SOME EXTRAORDINARY EVENTS

Children are not the only witnesses of miracles. In addition to those who were healed, many people witnessed extraordinary events. In 1981, it was particularly common for all the pilgrims to have mass visions.

4.7 SUN DANCE IN MEDJUGORJE

The phenomenon of the dance of the sun occurred not only in Fatima, but also in Medjugorje. On August 2, 1981, the feast of Our Lady of the Angels, in the late afternoon, before sunset, the sun began to rotate on its axis, approaching the spectators and then moving backwards. About one hundred and fifty people were able to look at the sun without harming their eyes. Some claim to have seen the Virgin, the Sacred Heart of Jesus and a large number of angels with trumpets coming out of the sun. At the end, a white cloud covered the hill of the first apparition, the sun approached and then returned to its place as if nothing had happened. All this took about fifteen minutes. After this event, it has happened several times recently to different pilgrims. I recommend you to search on youtube or tiktok "the dance of the sun" and you will see some videos from the year 2021 and 2023 where this event happened again and you can feel the warmth of God and see with your own eyes the miracles that Medjugorje has shown us. This fact is very strong for our faith and I hope that yours and mine will be strengthened.

4.8 THE CROSS

The following text is taken from the book "The Apparitions of Medjugorje" by Svetozar Kraljevic: "The author of these lines has seen the cross on the hill Krizevac transformed into a pillar of light that stood between heaven and earth, on the top of the hill. Many, many other people have seen the same thing. He added the testimony of those who saw the horizontal part of the cross and the lower part turn white and form the letter "T". Other people claim to have seen the luminous form of a woman instead of the cross."

4.9 AN UNKNOWN FIRE

On October 28, 1981, a fire of unknown origin broke out at the site of the first apparition. The fire burned for approximately fifteen minutes. Several hundred people saw it. The fire burned without consuming anything.

Then Our Lady said to the visionaries, "This is one of the preliminary signs of the great sign. All the signs are given to strengthen your faith until the final sign appears."

4.10   MIR

Shortly after Our Lady prayed for peace, a large inscription appeared in the sky above Krizevac Hill: the word MIR, Croatian for PEACE.

This happened one evening in July 1981. The visionaries testify that Our Lady promised that there would be more breakthrough signs in Medjugorje and in other parts of the world before the great sign.

CHAPTER 5: COMMENTS FROM VARIOUS RELIGIOUS

5.1 THE GREATEST MESSAGE: THE APPARITION OF MARY. VARIOUS COMMENTS BY FR. SVETOZAR KRALJEVIC

"For me personally, the greatest message of Medjugorje is the apparition of Mary herself. For the visionaries, she has become visible and tangible. They listen to her, talk to her, sing and pray with her. Heaven is opened to us through Mary. All that Jesus spoke to us about is true, it has become tangible. In a person who receives this faith, everything takes on a new meaning and a new birth is experienced. That is why, through her apparition, Mary gives birth to the Church."

5.2 FR. MICHAEL SCANLAN

"I received a very deep and very strong sense of Mary's presence, and on a spiritual level I felt that Mary was asking me to keep these children in the depths of my heart.

I also felt the inner emotion of being strong in faith and believing in the supernatural nature of what I saw. "I have witnessed a faith and spiritual fervor in the liturgies here that is far greater than in any other parish liturgy I have been able to attend in the world. The closest expression of faith is the Blessing of the Blessed Sacrament in Lourdes."

5.3 HANS URS VON BALTHASAR (FAMOUS THEOLOGIAN, APPOINTED CARDINAL, DIED IN JUNE 1988 AT THE AGE OF 82).

"Mary's exhortations, messages and petitions to the faithful become more and more concrete. Our Lady is the prototype of the Church, the Church in its purest form, the Church as it should be. Mary is not a private person. One could say that she is a universal person. Precisely because she is perfectly humble, she appears with a rosary in her hand and presents herself as a mediator before her Son."

5.4 DAVID DUPLESSIS (LEADING PROTESTANT IN THE UNITED STATES).

"In spite of so many contacts with the Catholic Church, I have never experienced such a spirit of prayer as now in Medjugorje. The Catholic tradition about the Virgin Mary bothered me for a long time; when I came to Medjugorje, I thought that I would only hear about Mary, but instead, the name that was mentioned most often was that of Jesus. The Catholics taught me that the Virgin Mary leads us to Christ."

5.5 A MUSLIM DERVISH

"I felt so much joy in my heart that I wanted to scream. I thought that I too would fall into ecstasy (by helping in the apparition room and living the moment of the apparition with the visionaries) and I decided to spend the whole night in prayer. These people are searching for God. When they seek Him, they find Him. When they find Him, they possess Him lovingly, and whoever is in love with God, nothing can separate them from His love."

5.6 ANOTHER MUSLIM

"When I saw the church of Medjugorje, I fell on my knees and thanked Our Lady for calling me to this place. I became convinced that the God of Christians is also my God, and that the Virgin Mary is not only the Mother of Catholics, but also my Mother."

5.7 FR. STANKO VASILJ

"Never in the history of the Church has Our Lady been so close to people as she is here in Medjugorje, not only to the visionaries, but to all people, to all humanity. None of us can imagine the importance and the mercy that God has given us by sending His Mother here. She came to this oasis of faith in the midst of the desert of unbelief that reigns everywhere today, to revive our faith, to make rivers of grace gush forth for the whole world, to transform it into a flowering orchard of God."

5.8 CZECHOSLOVAK BISHOP PAOLO HNILICA

"The phenomenon of Medjugorje has become an international phenomenon and we cannot pass by it with indifference. The silence of the Church must be interpreted positively: So far, all is well. For the faithful, signs like Medjugorje are an encouragement, a motivation to open themselves inwardly to God. In Fatima, the Mother of God, through her children, speaks to those who also believe, pray and love God. She invites us to pray for others, for those who do not believe, for sinners. God wants to give us all His mercy, but we, wise and intelligent people, are not able to accept it because we are not able to understand it.

That is why Our Lady almost always appears to children. Only the simple can understand the true meaning of the Lord's words and live them in their hearts.

The great theologian and all of us, priests of God, often behave like the Pharisees: we are custodians of the law and we know it well, and this knowledge is not necessary for salvation. Again, the word of the Lord is clear: "Unless you become as little children, you will not enter the kingdom of God" (Mt 18:3). (Mt 18:3)".

The task of the priest before the apparitions of Medjugorje is therefore to imitate Mary, who "pondered everything in her heart" and grew in knowledge and discernment, praying and always doing the will of God. Priests, and even more so the faithful, must pray, fast and convert, not only because it is demanded by Jesus in the Gospel. In fact, only a solid communion with God can give us the necessary light to accomplish what Providence has entrusted to us.

The Virgin Mary, among angels, saints and men, was the only one found worthy to become the Mother of God and to educate and guide Jesus. Mary, then, is the way that the Lord shows us today, more than ever, as sure and true.

By placing ourselves in the arms of this Mother, by consecrating ourselves to her, as St. Louis de Montfort wisely taught us, we will change the world. Jesus, through Mary, sent the Holy Spirit to those gathered with her in the Cenacle. Surely no one will be able to reach God without passing through the Immaculate Heart of the Virgin."

5.9 RENE LAURETIN (FAMOUS THEOLOGIAN):

"The present moment is manifesting new and significant effects. Apparitions have always been part of the life of the Church. Most of the apparitions I have studied have a local and private character; they are bound to a time and a place.

It is a prophetic cry from heaven that brings its fruits to its rightful place.

Medjugorje, on the other hand, where the message has a worldwide reach and audience, is an exception. As far as the content is concerned, in general we find an extraordinary convergence.

These apparitions make a diagnosis and sound an alarm: the inhabitants of the world have quietly and joyfully given themselves over to sin. People are digging the pit, it is self-destructing.

But beware, this is not God's punishment or vengeance. It is a justice inherent in sin itself. In a world well made by God, sin is destructive; drug addiction, war, AIDS, do not come from God.

Sin offends God and fills our mother's face with tears, and that is the most terrible thing, more than the consequences of sin itself. As for Jos's cure, it is simple: it is the message of the Gospel that we have forgotten too much.

The apparitions take up this message of the Gospel from its beginning, that is, from the preaching of John the

Baptist; return to God, conversion, penance, prayer, reconciliation, peace."

CHAPTER 6: THE MOST RECENT AND IMPRESSIVE MESSAGES OF OUR LADY IN MEDJUGORJE

Since January 8, 1987, Our Lady has given a special message on the 25th of each month. Before that, since March 1984, they were received every Thursday. I personally follow the messages of the Virgin Mary every month, which are published on various websites and social networks. Each time I read them, I am filled with faith, hope, serenity, harmony and above all peace. Below I will present you with the most important messages that Our Lady has sent in Medjugorje in recent times, but there are so many messages that Our Lady has sent that I could not write them all in this book, but I promise you that I will try to make a compilation of them all, because I believe that each message is a reason for hope for every person in this world. I recommend that you share these messages and the information in this book with your closest family and friends, because the Virgin Mary invites us to take her messages to the world for the salvation of our souls.

6.1 MESSAGE, JANUARY 25, 2023

"Dear children! Pray with me for peace, because Satan wants war and hatred in hearts and among nations. Therefore, pray and sacrifice your days in fasting and penance so that God may give you peace. The future is at a crossroads because modern man does not want God. That is why mankind is heading for destruction. You, little children, are my hope. Pray with me that what I began in Fatima and here may become a reality. Pray and witness to peace in your surroundings and be people of peace. Thank you for responding to my call."

6.2 MESSAGE, FEBRUARY 25, 2023

"Dear children! Convert and clothe yourselves with penitential garments and deep personal prayer, humbly asking the Most High for peace. In this time of grace, Satan wants to seduce you, but you, little children, look at my Son and follow Him to Calvary in renunciation and fasting. I am with you because the Most High allows me to love you and lead you to the joy of the heart in the faith that grows in all those who love God above all. Thank you for responding to my call". Date: 18.03.2023. The visionary Mirjana Dragicevic - Soldo had daily apparitions from June 24, 1981 to December 25, 1982. On the last day of the apparition, after having confided to her the tenth secret, Our Lady told her that throughout her life she would have an apparition once a year - on March 18. This has been the case all these years and this year as well. The apparition began at 13:33 and lasted until 13:39."

6.3 MESSAGE, MARCH 18, 2023 - ANNUAL APPEARANCE TO MIRJANA SOLDO

"Dear children, through prayer and mercy I invite you to know my Son as much as possible; that with pure and open hearts you may learn to listen; that you may hear what my Son is saying to you so that you may come to see spiritually. May they, as one people of God, in communion with my Son, bear witness to the truth by their lives. Pray, my children, that together with my Son you may bring only peace, joy and love to all your brothers and sisters. I am with you and I bless you with my motherly blessing."

6.4 MESSAGE, MARCH 25, 2023

"Dear children! May this be a time of prayer for you."

6.5 MESSAGE, APRIL 25, 2023

" Dear children! I invite you all to be bearers of the peace and joy of the Risen Jesus for all those who are far from prayer, so that the love of Jesus may transform them through their lives to a new life of conversion and holiness. Thank you for responding to my call."

6.6 MESSAGE, MAY 25, 2023

" Dear children! I invite you to go out into nature and pray that the Most High may speak to your heart and that you may feel the power of the Holy Spirit so that you may bear witness to the love that God has for every creature.

I am with you and I intercede for you. Thank you for responding to my call. Thank you for answering my call."

6.7 MESSAGE, JUNE 25, 2023

" Dear children! The Most High allows me to be in your midst, to pray for you, to be your mother and your refuge. Little children, I invite you to return to God and to prayer, and God will bless you abundantly. Thank you for responding to my call."

6.8 MESSAGE, JULY 25, 2023

" Dear children! In this time of grace in which the Most High sends me to you to love you and to lead you on the path of conversion, offer your prayers and sacrifices for all those who are far away and have not known the love of God. You, little children, be witnesses of love and peace to all troubled hearts. Thank you for responding to my call."

6.9 MESSAGE, AUGUST 25, 2023

" Dear children! In this time of grace I invite you to pray with your heart. May your hearts, little children, rise to heaven in prayer so that your heart may feel the God of Love who heals you and loves you with an immense love. This is why I am with you to lead you on the path of conversion of heart. Thank you for responding to my call. "

6.10 MESSAGE, SEPTEMBER 25, 2023

" Dear children, I invite you to a powerful prayer. Modernism wants to invade your thoughts and rob you of the joy of prayer and of the encounter with Jesus. Therefore, my dear little children, renew prayer in your families so that my motherly heart may rejoice as in the first days when I chose you and the answer was prayer day and night and Heaven did not remain silent but granted peace and blessings in abundance to this place of grace. Thank you for answering my call."

6.11   MESSAGE, OCTOBER 25, 2023

" Dear children, the winds of evil, hatred and tribulation are blowing over the earth to destroy life. Therefore, the Most High has sent Me to you to lead you on the path of peace and unity with God and mankind. You, little children, are my outstretched hands: pray, fast and offer sacrifices for peace, the treasure for which every heart longs. Thank you for responding to my call."

6.12   MESSAGE, NOVEMBER 25, 2023

" Dear children! May this time be interwoven with prayer for peace and good works, so that the joy of waiting for the King of Peace may be felt in your hearts, in your families and in the world that has no hope. Thank you for responding to my call. "

6.13   DECEMBER 25, 2023 - ANNUAL APPEARANCE TO JAKOV

In the last daily apparition on September 12, 1998, Our Lady told Jakov Colo that he would have an apparition every year on December 25. This was also the case this year. Our Lady came with the Child Jesus in her arms. The apparition began at 2:20 p.m. and lasted 6 minutes.

"Dear children, today, with my Son in my arms, I want to invite you all to pray to the Child Jesus for the healing of your hearts. Children, sin often reigns in your hearts and destroys your lives, and you cannot feel the presence of God. Therefore, today, on this day of grace when grace is being spread throughout the world, give your life and your heart to the Lord so that He may heal you with His grace. Only with a pure heart will you be able to experience the rebirth of Jesus in you and the light of His birth will illuminate your life. I bless you with my motherly blessing. Thank you for responding to my call."

6.14   MESSAGE, DECEMBER 25, 2023

"Dear children! I bring you My Son Jesus to fill your hearts with peace, for He is peace. Little children, seek Jesus in the silence of your heart so that He may be reborn. The world needs Jesus, therefore, little children, seek Him in prayer, for He gives Himself daily to each one of you. "

Today Our Lady came dressed for a feast and with the Child Jesus in her arms. Jesus extended his hand in blessing and Our Lady prayed over us in the Aramaic language."

6.15 LAST MESSAGE, JANUARY 25, 2024

"Dear children! Let this time be a time of prayer. "

CHAPTER 7: SOME ADDITIONAL REFLECTIONS OF PRIESTS NEAR MEDJUGORJE

7.1 MEDITATIONS OF FR. TOMISLAV VIASIC ON THE MESSAGES OF MEDJUGORJE

Make the effort to pray, to live the sacraments, and you will discover the power of the messages. Pray, devote time to God, do not just read the prayers, you have to feel them. When I have to meet God, I place myself before Him and I don't begin to pray "Our Father", but I place myself before the Father like a child:

"I am suffering now, I have a headache, I am tense, help me, I have these problems". If we want to start a path to get to God, let's not start with the prayer that is already determined, but let's start to go to God to get to the prayer. Many people say prayers, but they do not seek God.

"Today I am depressed, I have so many difficulties, I cannot be at peace before You, help me! If we make this way to reach God, our prayers will become an encounter with God.

I want to bring you to the level of life, to the spiritual level, where you can accept the message and live it. The peace to which Our Lady calls is an inner, spiritual peace, from which all other peace, all well-being, comes. Our Lady says precisely: "WHEN YOU THINK OF EVIL, OF PUNISHMENTS, OF WARS, YOU ARE ON THE WAY TO ERROR. YOUR DUTY IS TO ACCEPT, LIVE AND SPREAD DIVINE PEACE!

When we allow God to change our life, everything becomes easier, our life receives a peace from which is born a gift of joy and gratitude, of recognition and love. If you feel united to God and to the Blessed Mother, if you feel responsible for the Kingdom of God, then you have to pray, you have to increase your prayer, you have to put God first every day in your family, before the television, before the game.

Jesus says that it is necessary to love one's enemies, and I have understood that the fundamental thing in the spiritual life is to have strength, to feel the divine strength inside, to be stronger than all the obstacles, than all the enemies, than these shocks, than slander, than poverty, we have to be strong.

If we lack divine strength, we are destroyers of the people around us. How can we live that strength? How can we have that strength? I know how to have it; you know it too. Jesus retired all night to pray and then he acted. It seems to me that at this time we cannot pray all night like Jesus, but I believe that we must find a way to pray all day long: to be with Jesus and to continue to strengthen our inner life. If you want to progress in the spiritual life, if you want to be strengthened every day by all your prayers, you have to take two steps.

7.1.1 THE FIRST STEP TO IMPROVE OUR SPIRITUAL LIFE: BECOME AWARE OF MY UNREDEEMED PART.

I am nervous, I have no peace with anyone, I am angry, I am bitter, I am worried: I must always keep my unredeemed part before my spiritual eyes, let others know this part, let them really know it so that they can help me. This step is very important so that our prayers are not formulas, but a search for God who saves from the depths of our unsaved being.

7.1.2 THE SECOND STEP. FORGIVE.

Christian forgiveness is to love because I am blessed and my joy, my understanding, my love goes beyond that because I am full of power, full of life. When I am full of God, I understand all situations, I understand everyone. I understand, I understand and I accept when I am slandered, when I am persecuted, when I am poor? We have to overcome the bitterness, the impatience, the slander, the insults. To overcome. To overcome means to live salvation and to save others.

In my opinion, these two steps should always be present in our life: when we pray, when we are on the path of our daily life, when we are in contact with God. Every day we must cry out from the depths of our unredeemed being and go in search of the face of the Lord, to discover Him and to go towards forgiveness. This is the only way to increase inner strength, and when inner strength increases, this happens at the same time: people are converted. Our Lady does not appear by chance, not like any other saint, but Our Lady has a special mission in the Church, for the salvation of each one of us. Our Lady asks for conversion, and who needs to be converted? We all need to be converted. Neither the wise nor the best are converted yet. We all have to go forward and participate in the life of God through the trials of life. When we are ready to adore God with joy, to jump for joy when we are tested, when we are poor, when we are slandered, to suffer everything in peace and joy, then we are on the way to conversion, then we are mature to live a life with God. Our Lady asks us to accept the messages. The acceptance of the messages is precisely this new life that makes the face of God shine, the face of Our Lady on our face.

And we can only be authentic messengers if we become a Church in which the face of God is manifested. Do not look for Our Lady and her messages on the level of new truths, it is a mistake; look for them only on the level of new dynamics, Our Lady, as I said, wants to awaken us so that we can see, hear, feel with the heart.

We should be interested in knowing what God wants from us, what we should do for God, how we can offer our life to God, how we can offer our sickness to God... .... We have to enter into the heart of Jesus. We must decide to live for God, with God, in God, moving in God.

7.2 THE ROSARY AND PRAYER

The novelty of the Rosary is its contemplation. The Rosary is a beautiful prayer when it is contemplated, when Scripture is placed before each mystery, when it follows the life of Jesus and the life of our redemption. Then you can always go forward, but with an ever more open heart, with an ever greater recollection. Have this recollection in your homes, in your hearts, in your groups, and you will see that things go well. Prayer. The most useful thing for everyone will be prayer. Be a constant time of prayer. Hold the rosary in your hands and also hold your heart in it. I have never understood as I understand now that you cannot enlighten people's minds with human arguments, with human logic, but only with the supernatural power that God gives us. So I ask you: abandon yourselves to the Immaculate Heart and live an immaculate attitude. Our Lady has called us to live a communitarian prayer:

Without us, we can live communal prayer, we can do everything. First of all, to find the time to pray in our families, then more deeply, to be united in the Spirit at all times. Everything that is done with Our Lady receives more strength and the way with Her becomes easier. There is a group in Medjugorje that is guided by Our Lady. In this group I have never encountered the difficulties and problems that are found in other groups: certain fanaticisms, certain quarrels, envy; I have never encountered them. There is simplicity, harmony and peace. Our Lady said: "If you want to be happy, live a simple, humble life, pray a lot and do not go into the depths of problems, let God solve them. I recommend to you: "Clean your houses well, because they are complicated, you have too many things, and you have no time for yourselves or for God, because you make your life complicated. Give to the poor and you will be able to pray. It is necessary to give and open your hearts. It is useless, you will be destroyed by the rhythm of life of your cities, if you do not organize your interior, your intimate life, if you do not organize your homes, your families, so that a divine rhythm, of God, reigns. Only when you organize this inner rhythm will you be stronger than the rhythm of the cities, a rhythm that drags you down and destroys you. Our Lady says: "All adults have the capacity to know that God exists. The sin of the world is that they are not interested in God. The cities, the regions are full of churches and mosques, but people do not go there to ask: "How should I live? Prayer comes by praying. Not with the theory of prayer. It comes by praying, like appetite comes by eating. To say, "I don't know how to pray," doesn't mean you can't start. I must find the time, take the Bible, the Rosary. Start and you will see! If we stay on the level of asking for things, we are not praying. To pray is to dedicate a space of time, as we dedicate it to a friend who comes to visit us, and not to be interrupted until we have finished our conversation with him or the time we have dedicated to him. So it is with prayer. If you want to pray in this way, Our Lady will show herself little by little; prayer is being close to the Lord.

That is why Our Lady asks us for the Creed, the confirmation of our faith. Our Lady makes a more radical school, more bearable. Radical, not to take up our time with prayer or to make us live on bread, but to prepare us.

Prayer and fasting are indispensable means to have peace, to have faith and to be able to give ourselves. We can delay or hasten the triumph of Our Lady, it depends on us.

We are all responsible for the salvation of souls.

7.3 IF WE DO NOT UNDERSTAND THE CROSS, WE WILL NEVER UNDERSTAND ANYTHING ABOUT CHRISTIAN LIFE (COMMENTS BY FR. SLAVKO BARBARIC - 1984)

Our Lady wants to lead us to the cross. In one of her messages, the Virgin Mary said: "PRAY MUCH FOR PEACE, IN FRONT OF THE CROSS". The Cross is a precious word, the greatest word that the Lord could say to us. What does it mean, the cross of sickness, the cross of suffering? If we do not understand the cross, we will never understand anything about the spiritual life; we will not understand anything about the life of Jesus. Our Lady, as a humble and poor servant before the Lord, waited for the Servant of the Lord. To be able to be the Mother of God, she had to understand the Cross. And she wants us to understand the Cross as well. Do you see how much the visionaries suffer? It is a suffering for Jakov to live without a father, without a mother; for Ivanka, too; for Vicka with her illness and her burns. I see that there is suffering in their lives, but in a different form. They carry the cross with joy. This is what Our Lady wants us to learn. We will not be saved by our cross, by our suffering, but the Lord will give us strength. Our Lady, like Jesus, did not come to remove all suffering from the world, but to teach us how to live with suffering. As the Apostle says: For those who love the Lord, all suffering is good. And often, with our lives, before the cross, in our homes, we do so many things that are not good!

Our Lady also wants to lead us to a poor life when she asks us to fast. She does not ask us to go hungry, she asks us to go deeper, to live a life purified from all evil, from all sin. A poor person believes that he can give himself, he will never put his hope in the material world or in anything earthly. A poor person will never say to anyone, "I have no need," he is open before the Lord and before other people. That is what counts. Our Lady knows this and that is why she asks us to fast on bread and water.

7.4 VICKA'S SEVERE BURN

"Our Lady taught me to offer all my sicknesses and sufferings to her Son for the conversion of sinners," said the visionary Vicka.

In the fire caused by the stove, the flames penetrated the entire kitchen of Vicka's house. The visionary was outside talking to some pilgrims. Warned of the danger, she went into the kitchen to save her little nephews and nieces who were inside. Vicka had burns all over her face and one hand. While we were taking her to the hospital in Mostar," says Ana (Vicka's sister), "my sister was singing 'Maria..... Maria...'" Her mother, who was with her, said, "Vicka is crazy, how can she sing?" The same thing was said by the doctors in Mostar, who did not know where to put their hands, so battered was the poor creature. Her face was black as coal, her eyes almost closed, her lips swollen and puffy. She was disfigured. But she never lost her beautiful smile, her peace and her singing. "It is easy," she said, "to sing when one is well, but it is much more beautiful to sing when one is suffering. If God wants it that way, it's okay, I'm not going to ask Him why. He knows what is best for me.

The pilgrims thought: "Vicka does not want to be seen because she looks like a monster", but she went out as soon as she saw that people were there, even though she was bandaged.

7.5 THE BOY'S FIVE LOAVES

The 5 loaves seemed small in the hands of the boy in the Gospel (Matthew 14:17-21), and they were multiplied in the hands of Jesus. The 5 mysteries of the Rosary, which seem so small to you, are not small in the hands of Our Lady. The 5 loaves of the Gospel reached 5,000 people; your prayer can reach 5 million; every time you pray, a miracle happens. Our Lady wants to put 5 loaves in each pilgrim's bag: prayer, fasting, the Eucharist, the Bible and monthly confession.

7.6 FR. JOZO'S RELIGIOUS EXPERIENCE
7.6.1 Parish Priest's incredulity

At the beginning of the apparitions, I was a parish priest in Medjugorje and I did not believe in them. At first I was very worried, and then I was very afraid. I was afraid that they were the lies of children, manipulated by atheists to ridicule religion and the Christian faith. In fact, after the war, on several occasions, they tried to organize religious scenes with lighthouses and lights to make people believe that it was something supernatural and then tell them: "This is where the faith is based!

I was visited by some priest friends of mine: they watched, commented and then returned home saying: "Let him do it, it's not up to us". And they left me alone. One day the parish priest of Liubuski came with two other priests and told me: "I think the boys are possessed.

7.6.2   THE BISHOP'S FAITH

At that time my bishop from Mostar also came. He wanted to see the visionaries, and before he asked them some questions, he asked them to swear to him the truth. Then he talked with them for quite a long time, first with each one of them and at the end with all of them together. I was outside, very nervous. When the bishop came out, he told me that it seemed to him that the boys were telling the truth and that it was up to us to believe and do what the messages said. "What more do you need to believe? -Monsignor Zanic said. I am sure, I have not the slightest doubt.

I, on the other hand, remained unbelieving and answered him: "It is necessary that we go slowly. We have the Revelation, we have Christ, we have the Church. Tomorrow it could turn out to be an illusion and we would be ashamed". But the bishop insisted: "I am sure, I do not need to investigate. And he was even irritated by my skepticism. I remained incredulous, but I did not stop talking to the visionaries every day, writing down their words, and analyzing them at night. If something did not seem logical to me, I would question the visionaries the next day. One day they told me that Our Lady would appear in the Church.

I was happy because I thought that in that case people would go to the hill and find nothing and no one, be disappointed, and everything would be over. But they immediately had the answer for me: "Don't worry. Whoever called them to the hill before will know how to call them to the church now.

Indeed, the next day, by noon, the church was completely full. I walked in and all I could see were heads. It was 6 o'clock in the evening and I was getting ready to celebrate Mass.

7.6.3   PRAY THE ROSARY EVERY DAY

The sermon was unfortunate. I told them that the parish was going through a serious crisis and that curiosity was prevailing. "After the death of the last apostle," I said, "we do not need any more revelations. Jesus has told us all he has to tell us. Heaven has spoken, period. We have the Bible, we have Christ, we have the Church, and that is enough for us. Why are you still disobedient? Jesus said, "Believe not when they say unto you, Behold, behold..." My sermon lasted about half an hour, but it did not convince anyone. In fact, the people were nervous.

I wanted to finish the Mass soon; a Mass that was very sad, like an insult to the parishioners; not an offering, not a change, not a grace. I had my hands on the altar and was preparing to kiss it, to say goodbye, when I felt someone pulling me towards the dawn, inclining me to kiss the altar, I looked out of the corner of my eye to see who it was: it was Jakov. He waved his finger at me because he wanted to tell me something. He murmured, "I have a message for the whole town.

Jakov was 10 years old, very small and could not reach the fixed microphone. So I grabbed him by the armpits and stood him up on the altar. Jakov shouted at the top of his lungs: Our Lady said, "Pray the Rosary every day; pray together." The response was a tremendous and long applause.

I looked at this child, who came to catechesis with the other 350 children of the parish, and I thought that perhaps this message from him came from his catechetical experience. I didn't think it was a message. The words were too simple to be a message from heaven. I looked at the people who were now crying their eyes out, and I said to the Lord, "I don't understand anything! Why are they crying now?"

7.6.4   OUR LADY'S RESPONSE

I walked slowly to the sacristy and waited for the people to leave. After taking off my vestments, I returned to the presbytery: everyone was there, in their place, with the rosary in their hands. No one had moved. They seemed as motionless as the trees in the forest. Then I also took out my rosary and began to pray with them. After a long time, it was already night, and suddenly the temple was illuminated with a great light and Our Lady appeared in the middle of the temple, above the people.

With a sweet and clear voice she said "Pray the Rosary every day; pray together. These were the same words that Jakov had said to all those present two and a half hours earlier. Our Lady did not say this for Jakov, who had already received this message, nor for the parishioners who had believed and stayed to pray with tears. Our Lady said it to me so that I, as a priest and pastor, would believe.

From that day on, the people continued to pray the Rosary every day in the church and in their families. There was a change of personnel in the parish because new Franciscans arrived.

Perhaps some of the friars thought it would be better to replace the Rosary with another prayer. But they could not say this out loud, because it was not possible to go against the message of Our Lady, against the presence of the "Gospa" who had said to all the parishioners: "Pray the Rosary every day, pray together!"

7.6.5   ONLY ONE DAY...

Since that day, the Rosary has been prayed every day in the Church. Just one day...just one day, August 17, 1981, the call of the Blessed Mother was on the verge of not being fulfilled. In the morning, very early in the morning, large contingents of police and troops began to arrive in military cars and trucks, all in a state of war, while helicopters flew overhead in the sky of Medjugorje. They cordoned off and blocked all the entrances to the village, so that no one could enter or leave Medjugorje. They came with the order to destroy "the myth of Medjugorje".

Shortly afterwards, hundreds of pilgrims began to arrive from all over the world. Two days earlier, on August 15th, more than 25,000 people had been counted, among them many priests who had come to hear confessions. Now, facing the barrier of soldiers and policemen with guns in their hands and dogs on leashes, the pilgrims, without protesting, knelt down in the direction of the church and began to pray the rosary. No one wanted to go home. The people were not afraid.

Our Lady had told them through the visionaries: "Do not be afraid. You will not be able to close the church. Just pray and bear witness to me". It was not a strike, the people were not protesting, they were not shouting, they were just praying, and they were children, adults, the elderly and even the sick....

7.6.6   BUT, 5 MINUTES BEFORE 6...

Some employees of the Secretariat of Internal Affairs entered the parsonage to search it, while some policemen took me prisoner. When people saw me leaving in the police car, they began to cry. At that moment everyone thought: "Medjugorje is over, today Medjugorje will be destroyed".

But the faithful did not lose heart, they continued to pray all day long under the scorching August sun. In prison I learned how it ended. Five minutes before 6 o'clock that evening, an order came from the government: "Let the people enter the church of Medjugorje. The gates were opened and a wave of people from all sides entered the church. The church and the courtyard were filled to overflowing, and the community spent the whole night in the church, praying, singing, and crying.

7.6.7 THE GREAT LESSON

On that day, we believers learned that the Christian on earth is the strongest soldier in the world when he has the Rosary in his hands. On that day, once again, the woman clothed in the sun crushed the head of the infernal serpent. The Church sang victory, not by diplomacy with the atheists who wanted to crush us, but by following Our Lady's message: "Pray the Rosary".

Why did Our Lady mention the Rosary? Because it is the biography of Jesus, the "curriculum" of the life of Jesus that has not yet been written. The Gospels have not finished writing the life of Jesus, because Jesus continues to live in us and continues to complete his life in us. That is why Our Lady wants the Rosary to return to our churches and to our families. If you need peace, you will find it in the Rosary; if you need faith, health, joy, love, you will find it in prayer.

7.7 QUESTIONS TO FR. PETAR LJUBICIC

What testimony can you give us about the apparitions in Medjugorje?

Fr. Petar: For me, these apparitions mean that God is alive and wants to save mankind. Even though there is so much evil and great sin on this earth, God continues to give His love to the world. These apparitions could have lasted a few months, like Lourdes and Fatima. But since the world has forgotten God so much, I think God is extending the time of our salvation and sending us His Mother to help us return to Him. God is waiting for a person who has not confessed for 30 or 40 years, which means that God is waiting for us with love to save us. When these people come to Medjugorje, they say: "I have nothing to be ashamed of here, because Our Lady is my mother and I have nothing to hide". Others say: "These apparitions convince us that we cannot continue to live in sin as we have been doing.

We know that Mirjana will announce an extraordinary event to you three days in advance, does this fact make you serene or does it create anxiety?

Fr. Petar: Our Lady does not want to frighten anyone. She just wants us to prepare ourselves so that later, when it is too late, we will not be frightened. What will happen? We do not know, because it is a secret: it is certain that it is something unpleasant, especially for those who play with the salvation of their souls. Once, through Mirjana, Our Lady said: "Many are interested in these things only when they are going to happen; I have been here for 5 years calling for conversion and prayer.

This is the most important thing: when the time of fulfillment comes, there will be little time for reflection and conversion. If we do not accept these calls of the

Lord now, while we are waiting for the sign, we are in danger of not accepting the final call.

7.8 LIVING THE CONSECRATION TO MARY

Pope Pius XI wrote: "Consecration to the Blessed Virgin is a gift of self for time and eternity. It is a gift, not of mere formality or sentiment, but an effective gift, realized in the intensity of a Christian and Marian life". We know that consecration in itself is made only to God. It is God who sets apart and reserves persons or things for his service; but it can also be man who offers himself or his things to God. The first and most important "consecrated" is Christ, which in Greek means "anointed". Christians, too, are anointed and consecrated in baptism in imitation of Christ. In this way, the Christian in Christ becomes "God's own". In an articulated way, the priest, the bishop and, by their vows, the religious are "consecrated".

The form of devotional consecration that Our Lady asked of us in Fatima and now in Medjugorje is rather a "sacrifice", which means first of all to be a truly Christian soul. It is a commitment to live the Christian life with Mary as our model and to allow ourselves to be "modeled" by her. On the cross, Jesus entrusted to Mary the care of all people: "Behold your son" .... "Behold your mother. The soul that consecrates itself to Mary makes it easier for her to fulfill the maternal mission that she received at the foot of the Cross. That is why she said in Medjugorje: "Dear children, today I am very happy because many want to consecrate themselves to me; I thank you: you are not mistaken. My Son is also happy about your consecration". (17-5-1983).

Christ is the image of the Father; Mary was the most faithful disciple of Jesus; the soul who consecrates herself to Mary chooses - as St. Louis de Montfort affirms - the easiest, quickest and most perfect way to imitate Christ and to go to the Father. Our Lady said in Medjugorje on October 25, 1988, that the purpose of consecration to Our Lady is to better belong to God: "I invite you to consecrate yourselves to my Immaculate Heart; I want you to consecrate yourselves personally, as families and as parishes, so that you all belong to God through my hands. The soul consecrated to Mary is proud to belong to her and to repeat often the words of Montfort, which the Holy Father John Paul II has made his own: "I am all yours, O Mary, and all my things are yours."

7.9 THE ROSARIES ARE TURNING GOLDEN – FR. JOHN J. SZANPY NARRATES

"One day in the spring of 1987 I received a phone call. "Fr. John, have you heard the latest news from Medjugorje, that the rosaries are turning gold? I rejected this news, I replied, and I think that Satan is already beginning his tricks to distract the pilgrims from the core of the Marian messages: prayer, conversion, fasting, faith and peace.

I felt uneasy when I imagined so many pilgrims in Medjugorje, amazed by such events, wasting time with comments about golden rosaries and perhaps neglecting prayer, personal conversion and growth in faith. In August 1987, I went to Medjugorje for a 30-day spiritual retreat.

There were many people who told me about these little "miracles". Most of them were young people from various English-speaking countries, to whom I listened patiently, withholding my answers about the phenomenon. I was impressed by the fact that, contrary to what I had thought, these people did not dwell on their experiences, nor did they waste time talking about them.

It was a phenomenon that was accepted with respect and without exaggerated emotions, rather as a loving sign from God to inspire greater faith and trust, just like the phenomena of the sun and the illumination of the cross on Krisevac.

I did not want to give my opinion until the Spirit of Sarto gave me light and understanding. It was about discovering God's hidden purpose, the message for the good of our souls. As I read and prayed with the Bible, I was enlightened by the words of the Book of Wisdom, 3:5-6, which states: "After suffering small punishments, they will receive great benefits, because God tested them and found them worthy of Him; He tried them like gold in a crucible. The Wisdom text compares us to gold.

Gold is taken from the earth, mixed with impurities that are separated by fire, and pure gold comes out. Our soul, which is gold before God, has been mixed with the impurities of original sin and other sins and needs to go through a process of purification and transformation. How does the soul achieve this kind of purification? Through repentance, which is the beginning of the process of refining this gold we call the soul.

Jesus said: "Whoever does not take up his cross and follow me cannot be my disciple. Well, the Rosary is the symbol of our Christian life, which, through the joyful and painful mysteries, must reach the resurrection, the transformation of our soul. The cross in the rosary symbolizes our faith and our patience to take up our daily crosses. It is through the long rosary of daily problems and crosses, illnesses, fears and pains. God purifies us as through fire, God reminds us to begin to live His message of conversion.

Just as my rosary or your rosary is transformed from silver to gold, our souls must be transformed from lukewarm to fervent, from good to better. Through this phenomenon, God wants to tell us that we must enter into a period of purification if we want to be washed by His loving action. In these living Rosaries, we are called to strengthen our resolve by meditating on the mysteries of the Rosary and learning to adapt the example of the life of Jesus and Mary to our own daily lives.

In conclusion, the current transformation of the Rosary is nothing less than God's invitation to conversion, a personal message given to each of us to respond to, to allow for the purification of our souls and thus become worthy of the great plans God has for our future, thus ensuring our peace and happiness. Just before writing this (1988), my rosary turned "golden" and, faithful to His Word, I entered a period of new and unexpected difficulties; but the light and love of the Holy Spirit have plunged me into deep prayer and greater trust, able to understand God's purpose through the moments of purification He allows. I accept them as a precious gift of His grace that leads me to know and love Him more. Each time I pray, I look at the golden metal of my rosary, a glow that illuminates my spirit and reminds me that I am being purified to be holy and that my prayer life will support me and give me strength until the end, Hail Mary!

CHAPTER 8: SOME INTERVIEWS

8.1 INTERVIEW WITH JELENA VASILJ, WHO RECEIVES INSIDE VOICEOVERS

Jelena is Ivanka's neighbor, she was 10 years old when the apparitions began.

How do you see Our Lady?

I always see her when I pray and always inwardly.

What do you mean by inwardly?

I have never seen Our Lady physically, as a living person, but always in my soul.

Are you sure it is Our Lady?

Yes, because she speaks words that strike you and fill you with joy, and there comes a feeling of peace and joy that confirms to you that she is Our Lady.

When do you see her?

Usually in the afternoon, after Mass; sometimes during Communion.

Would you explain to us what the "prayer of the heart" is?

Our Lady has insisted that we pray with our hearts. That is, to always have the desire to pray. Not just out of habit, because others are praying, but because you feel the need to pray, the need for peace and help. Then, when you do something with your heart, you do it with love? It is a difficult feeling to explain.

Do you have any advice for us? Are there any thoughts we should share?

These are the things that seem important to me: Once we asked what things could others take home with them? He told us: "First of all, they should change their lives and their faith. Then the most important thing is not to take beautiful souvenirs. Our Lady said: "I did not come to make myself and Medjugorje known. She came to help us, to save us. She told us to pray always, it is fundamental for our life. May prayer be the light that illuminates our path when we walk in darkness. Above all, pray for inner peace, because she said that the most important thing is peace in our hearts.

In what year did you begin to receive the inner locutions and messages?

In 1982.

Is it true that this is the last time Our Lady will appear here on earth?

YES, IT IS TRUE.

In your opinion, what does the last time mean, that there will be no more apparitions? And why?

I ask myself the same question: Our Lady has told us: "You should not be afraid of anything, if you believe, if you know that Jesus is your friend and brother, why should you be afraid? If you believe, if you know that Jesus is your friend and brother, why should you be afraid?" When we believe, there is no fear.

So it seems that it is not necessary to be afraid. Is it also necessary to be confident?

Yes, because we all hope that the world will be saved. We pray for it. We cannot know what God will do in us, and we can help a lot with our prayers.

Is it necessary to realize that it is often difficult to do His will?

If we do not pray, it is almost impossible. It is necessary to pray, otherwise faith becomes a thing like everything else. It is necessary to pray more. Give it more importance. Then our faith will grow. If we pray little, it always remains a fear, we lose our faith, because the devil is never at rest, he is always on the lookout. He is always looking for us. And if we do not pray, it is natural that he will disturb us.

Do you never get tired of praying? Do you always have the desire?

Prayer is a rest for me, and it should be for everyone. Our Lady told us to rest in prayer. Do not pray only and always for fear of God. The Lord wants to give us peace, security and joy.

Then why do we feel tired when we pray so much?

Perhaps it is because we do not feel God as a Father. Our God is a God in the clouds

What does Mass mean to you?

It is a great moment for all of us. The Lord comes very close to us. And the Blessed Mother said that during the Mass she is closer to all of us. She is always closer.

Is she closer during the Mass than during the apparitions to the visionaries?

Yes, she is. Holy Mass is a great thing. That's how you have to pray. Our Lady highly recommended the Holy Mass. She said it was very important.

What about Communion?

Yes, Our Lady said that the Mass is not complete without Communion.

What do you think about confession?

Confession also seems to me to be very important. I remember what Fr. Tomislav told us once, and Our Lady repeated it: If a person wants to grow in his spiritual life, he must go to confession often. Then Fr. Tomislav said,

"If we go to confession once a month, it may be that we have not yet come closer to God. It is necessary to feel the need to go to confession and not to wait for the month. I don't know why, but when I go to confession, I feel more free from everything. It helps me to grow.

How else do you advise us to pray; with formulas we have been taught or with the heart?

Both. Also, to dialog with your heart, like never forgetting the rosary or other formulas. It is a beautiful thing to be able to say to God: My Father; Our Father!

8.2 OUR LADY'S MESSAGE TO THE YOUTH OF THE WORLD

Through this visionary, the Queen of Peace sends a message to the youth of the world. My life in the family, in society, at school and with young people has not changed much; perhaps I live more consciously now. Certainly, many things have changed in my spiritual life, my mother says that I pray more now. When I was nine, ten, eleven years old, when it was easier to turn away from God, the Blessed Mother protected me. Lately, Our Lady has been crying a lot, especially for young people, because they have gone away from God. She said that Satan is very powerful, that he wants to destroy his plans and that it is necessary to pray a lot. What makes me happy is that I see the Blessed Mother as my mother, Jesus as my friend and brother, and God as my father. They are very close to me, they help me a lot and they give me a lot of joy. It has given me great joy to understand that God does not want me to go away from my friends, but that our friendship should be deeper, so that I can continue to tell them who God is for me and show them through my prayer. For me, Our Lady is a mother; near her I see an angel with the appearance of a child. On Mt. Krizevac I saw several angels, six or seven. When I want to talk to them, I cannot find the right words. Our Lady showed me Jesus on the cross and the resurrected Jesus. But my vision is different from the other visionaries; I see Our Lady with my heart, not with my eyes. First, I pray a lot and then I see her when I close my eyes. She said that she is very pleased with the young people when they pray, but that it is not nice that they leave the church immediately after Mass; they should stay a little longer to thank the Lord.

Our Lady wants to help young people to be saved; that is why she expects us to pray and fast a lot.

8.3 THE SAD SITUATION OF YOUNG PEOPLE IN THE WORLD

Once when Our Lady appeared to me (in the way I said before), I saw a light so strong that it even made my head hurt. Our Lady, through the light, told me twice: "Pray so that my love may spread throughout the world. Then I felt reborn. Our Lady repeated: "Pray. This will give you the strength to pray according to the intentions of the Queen of Peace. Something told me that this time I would have a sad vision, so I asked Our Lady not to show it to me that night because I did not want to go to bed sad, but She said: "You must see the misery of this world. Come, I will show you. Let's look at Africa: Then she showed me the people building mud houses. The children brought straw. Then I saw a mother with her child, she was crying because she had nothing to feed her child. The mother got up and went to ask another house if they had anything to eat. But they had nothing. The mother returned with her child who asked her, "Mother, why are we the only ones who are hungry?" The mother wept and the child died. Then Our Lady showed me Asia: there was a war there. I saw great ruins and one man killing another. It was terrible. Shots were fired and men were screaming in fear. Then she showed me America: I saw a boy and a girl, very young, smoking, and Our Lady explained to me that it was drugs; she showed me some people who were injecting themselves. I felt a great pain in my head when I saw a brother stabbing another brother in the heart. The victim was a soldier.

At the end, I saw some people praying and happy, and I felt a little relieved. Then Our Lady blessed everyone.

8.4 INTERVIEWING THE VISIONARIES
8.4.1   IVAN IVANKOVIC

Can a person be possessed by Satan without knowing it?

Usually, if the person is a little careless, the devil can enter more easily. That is why we must always pray. Prayer is the most effective weapon against the devil.

How do you see the Blessed Mother every day?

I always see her in three dimensions. With a gray dress, a white veil, black hair, pink cheekbones and blue eyes, and her feet always appear on a cloud.

How do you see Our Lady at this time, does she see that people are responding to her message? Many are responding, but most are only responding with words, without putting the messages into practice in their daily lives.

Is there any reason why Our Lady does not give more messages outside of the 25th of each month?

The message to the world is still on the 25th of every month.

How long do the apparitions last?

For me, every apparition is the same. If it seems like a minute to some, it can be up to half an hour for us. We cannot measure time.

Have you ever seen Our Lady cry?

Very few times.

8.4.2   VICKA

Vicka, we know that Our Lady is inviting us to conversion all the time and we do not respond as She expects, will She always be so patient with us?

Yes, She is the Mother of all of us and has a very great love for all of us. Now whether She will continue to be patient with us cannot be said exactly, it depends on each one of us. She says that she does not want any of her children to fall into sin.

Does Our Lady feel that we are responding to her messages?

People respond, but not enough, as Ella expects. They need to do more. She wants her requests to be taken to heart. She does not expect everything to be lived at once, but little by little. Always forward, never backward.

What do we do if we don't have this faith to move forward?

We have to pray to receive faith. If we do not have it, we can ask God for it. We may not feel it, but we must pray. Even if we don't feel it, we must continue to pray and move forward. Then it will be easier.

Of all the messages given by the Virgin Mary, which do you think are the most important that we must fulfill?

Prayer, conversion and peace.

What message can we give to young people?

Our Lady has said that through prayer everyone can discover what is due. If you follow Our Lady's messages, each one will discover what is right for him.

Have you ever seen Our Lady crying?

I haven't. She always seems happy to me.

Have you ever had an apparition of Jesus?

At Christmas (December 25th), Our Lady always comes with the Child Jesus in her arms. And also on Good Friday, some years ago, Our Lady came with Jesus. We saw Him half-bodied, crowned with thorns, with spittle and blood on His face. Our Lady showed Him to us so that we could see how many sufferings the Lord endured for us.

8.4.3   MARIA

What does Our Lady recommend to us as parents? What should we pass on to our children?

Our Lady says that first of all parents should pray with their children at home, and if necessary, even to the point of giving their lives for their conversion. That is, to do everything in their power for their conversion.

What is the message that Our Lady repeats to you most often?

The messages that Our Lady insists on the most are: peace, prayer, conversion, fasting, sacrifice and Holy Mass.

How do you see Our Lady?

When she comes, she always has a gray dress, a white halo, blue eyes, black hair, and a cloud at her feet on which she always rests. She also has a crown of stars on her head.

But what is she like?

Our Lady is so beautiful that words cannot describe her. Once we asked her why she is so beautiful and she said: "I am like this because I love you all.

Has Our Lady ever kissed you?

Yes, sometimes.

People are praying more now than before. Is Our Lady satisfied?

Our Lady said that more people are praying now and more often, but it is still not enough. We must continue to pray more.

Will the sign of Our Lady's departure be seen all over the world or only in Mediugorje?

The sign that she will leave will remain on the hill of apparitions (Podbordo). It will be seen only here.

Will the sign be seen only on the day of the apparition or will it be permanent?

The Virgin said that it will be possible to see and even touch it, of course it will be permanent.

How can we bring Mary's message to our separated Christian brothers and sisters who do not accept that she is the mediator of all graces?

Our Lady has spoken to us several times about this. She has said that we must pray for them. Many Protestants have also come here and they themselves have said that they feel Our Lady. It is like a child who has no mother (orphan). They themselves have felt that something is missing in their lives. They feel an emptiness.

Why do young people not come to Communion?

Our Lady simply says that we must pray for them as well. Prayer can help them all. Also, parents must teach their children the right way. They have to live a good Christian life, with prayer and going to church and the sacraments.

Do you have a general message for everyone?

May they live the messages of Our Lady. By your example, teach others to live them. Not only here in Medjugorje, but also when you return home.

8.4.4   ANOTHER INTERVIEW WITH VICKA

Why does Our Lady appear in Medjugorje?

She wants everyone in the world to be saved. She came to call everyone to listen to her messages and to convert (to convert means to leave sin). Our Lady wants those who do not hear Her messages to live them and thus help others to return to God.

Ivan once told me that Our Lady said that the souls in Purgatory are terribly lonely and that they can only see us when we pray for them, is this true?

Yes, it is true. We should pray for them a lot. Our prayers can save them and they can go to heaven. They are totally dependent on our prayers to be delivered from their sufferings. (The day when most souls are delivered from Purgatory to go to Heaven is Christmas Eve).

How can we protect ourselves from evil?

We should pray the Holy Rosary every day and wear something blessed.

Vicka, there are millions of people on earth who are not Catholics, who are not even Christians, what does Our Lady expect from them?

Let them pray. They have a religion. They have their own way of praying. Mary Most Holy is close to them and loves them just the same. The messages are also for them. There is only one God. It is man who has made the divisions.

8.4.5   JACOV

What can you tell us about the Blessed Mother?

She told me that she is the mother of every person on earth. Anyone who wants to can have her as their mother to guide and protect them on earth and take them to heaven. She wants us to change our lives. She is calling the whole world to return to God.

Do you go to Mass every day?

Yes, the Virgin Mary taught me to make the Mass the center of my life.

Do you have any advice for families?

If the family has money and many comforts, limit the use of luxurious, superfluous things, practice self-discipline and live in moderation. And above all, PRAY THE ROSARY DAILY.!

8.4.6   MIRJANA

What is your role as seers in these apparitions?

The six of us are not important. We are just like a telephone line through which God communicates with His people.

Why did Our Lady come?

She is our Mother and she wants all of us to believe and listen to her messages. She desires that by the time the secrets are revealed, there will be no more unbelievers.

Are we living in the end times?

That is part of the mysteries.

Should we be afraid of what might happen?

No way, I have seen heaven! Nothing on earth is worth a moment's worry. We are God's children! If they only realized how much the Lord loves us and what He has in store for us, people would live in great peace.

What do you suggest we do?

Pray especially during Mass and talk to non-believers so that they begin to live the messages of our Mother. This is a time of grace. And ask those who already believe to be a true example of Christian faith.

Do you want to share something special that you have learned from Our Lady?

Of course you do. Acknowledge God's presence in every beautiful thing on earth, thank God. Remember the Lord every day and talk to Him. Try to feel the immense love He has for each one of us.

Many people don't believe in evil, they don't believe that Satan exists, what can you tell us?

He does exist. I personally had a vision about it. He is the most evil and destructive force in all of creation. His presence is usually felt when there is confusion, disorder or conflict.

How do we overcome temptations?

Through prayer and fasting. When we pray, we are children of God. We should use holy water, blessed objects, and always pray.

8.4.7 ANOTHER INTERVIEW WITH MARIA

When is Our Lady's birthday?

It is August 5th. The Church celebrates it on December 8, so I celebrate it twice.

What should young people do?

They must obey the Ten Commandments and live a Christian life. We know that our life does not end here. Death is the beginning of our life in heaven. We must use our life on earth to prepare for heaven.

How can we prepare to go to heaven?

Pray to recognize God's will in our lives and accept it with love. Surrender yourselves to the Lord more and more, day by day.

Is it true that these are the last apparitions of the Virgin Mary on earth?

It's true.

You see Our Lady every year on the anniversary of the apparition (June 25), can you describe the apparition you had?

Our Lady was very beautiful. She had like gold around her dress and her veil. She told me about the third and fourth mysteries. She wants everyone to live the messages and especially to pray and fast. Fasting frees us from things, makes us free.

CHAPTER 9: TESTIMONIALS

9.1 THE GIRL STARTED TO RUN

The girl Megle Cuhna Silva, 5 years old, from Brasilia, was playing in the dining room when a 16-inch television fell on her chest from a height of two meters. The child's mother was a spiritualist and her father a practitioner; the paternal grandparents, who are very religious, called a friend who had just returned from Medjugorje. He placed a medal of the Queen of Peace on the chest of the bedridden girl and prayed with other friends for her healing. After the prayer, the girl stopped coughing, began to breathe normally, asked for food, and soon began to run and play as before. Her parents took her to the hospital, where new tests were done and a complete recovery of the pulmonary hematoma was declared (Dr. Celso Antonio Rodriguez Da Silva, pneumologist). Brasilia, 10-13-98, Fr. Juan Murazzo.

9.2 FROM WHEELCHAIR TO BIKE

On July 25, 1987, an American lady, Rita Klaus, accompanied by her husband and three children, came to the parish office in Medjugorje. A woman full of life, agile, with a serene look, she wanted to speak with the Franciscans to tell them about her case. "I wanted to become a nun and I entered a convent. In 1960, on the verge of taking my vows, I got a terrible case of measles and then multiple sclerosis and had to leave the convent. I was living in Evans, Pennsylvania; because of my job, I moved to another city, met my husband and got married. I admit that I was not right with him in not revealing my illness. When I had to tell him, he was so angry that he thought about divorce. One day in 1986, I read an article in "Readers Digest" about the facts of Medjugorje. One night I read Laurentin's book about the apparitions. After reading it, I wondered what I could do to honor Our Lady. I prayed constantly, but not for my healing. On June 18, in the middle of the night, I heard a voice say to me: "Why don't you pray for your healing? Then I began to pray like this: "Dear Virgin, Queen of Peace, I believe that you are appearing to the children of Medjugorje. Immediately I felt a current running through my whole body, and I felt a special warmth in the parts that hurt the most. Another day I went to school as usual in a wheelchair. When I came back, no one was home. With my crutches, without anyone's help, I got up from the chair and went upstairs, bent down to take off my shoes, and at that moment I realized that my legs were completely healed.

I threw away my crutches and started walking up and down the stairs, praising and glorifying God. When my husband and children arrived, they were beside themselves. I told them, "Jesus and Mary healed me. The doctors could not believe their eyes, but after they recognized me, they said there was no explanation. Now I am going to teach on a bicycle. My healing also helped my relatives (three brothers and two sisters), who had distanced themselves from the Church and the sacraments, to return to religious practice".

9.3 CURED OF MALIGNANT CANCER

When I returned from my Easter vacation in 1987, I was rushed to the hospital because of severe abdominal pain and underwent surgery for acute appendicitis on May 2. The surgeons found a thick layer of fat of about 25 centimeters, which upon analysis turned out to be a malignant cancer. The three biopsies, in different laboratories, gave the same result. With surgery, I was given only a few months to live. I decided to have the surgery. Mrs. Armida Ochoa, who had just returned from Medjugorje, offered me some holy water that she had brought with her. It was the fifth day of the operation and the first day I was at home. I wet myself with the water where I had been operated and I felt a very strong burning, an exaggerated reaction, as if I were burning inside. The doctors recognized me and, in disbelief, sent me directly to the Nuclear Medicine Department of the Guadalajara Medical Center. The results of the tests were negative, I was perfectly healthy. I thank the Virgin for that. I have all the films in which the malignant cancer is clearly visible, and all the reports signed by the doctors. J. Luis Santana López

9.4 GETTING UP AND WALKING

Agnes Huepel, from Münster, Germany, is a young woman in her thirties, tall, robust, blond, with short hair.

She comes to the Medjugorje Church every evening for the Holy Mass and stands. She was miraculously healed. She was in a wheelchair for twelve months after an accident that left her handicapped. She was in Medjugorje several times until one evening, during Mass, she heard a voice saying to her: "You have to get up and walk! She stood up and left her wheelchair in a corner. She felt different, both physically and spiritually. She returned to Germany, but no one believed her. She felt very bad and went back to Medjugorje and asked Our Lady for her people to believe. "There is no visible sign for a blind person," explained Fr. Jozo. "Those who are blind do not see, those who do not have faith do not understand what God is doing in His Church and in His creatures. Let us pray for the Church to see."

9.5 ANOTHER TESTIMONY

It all began in April of 1988, when I met a young man who was a lecturer on Our Lady's apparitions in Medjugorje. He told me about Our Lady's messages and I felt something very special in me. Then he showed me a picture of Our Lady with the Child and I confess that when I saw it I felt a great emotion and a great love. This picture gave me something special, because I was not very fond of praying or of praying the Rosary, but I don't know what happened; I felt an enormous desire to pray and I did it by praying the Rosary. I felt the presence of Our Lady. As a result of starting to pray the Rosary and wearing the scapular, my life changed and I became closer to God. The change that took place in my life was like a miracle because I had never believed in Mary and I denied why Catholics believed in her. I began to see life more beautiful every day, I learned to accept others, to give love and to take off the masks I used to wear; I felt more love for myself, I realized that God loves me". Nadia Angelica, Mexico.

9.6 THE KRIZEVAC SWEEPER

My name is John Peter, I am 38 years old and I have been in Medjugorje for 7 months. I have been taking drugs for 10 years. I started at the age of 17 with hashish, then heroin. I was ashamed of myself, I saw my parents slowly dying, and the most frightening thing was that I had no feelings for them. In March 1988, a friend of mine had just returned from Medjugorje, and she let me listen to a tape with the story of Oberto, a young drug addict from Genoa, who was cured in Medjugorje. In a few minutes I decided to go there, thinking that if Our Lady had healed Oberto, she would also heal me. I spent several sleepless nights in despair. I knew I was dead, but Our Lady gave me new life and cured my illness. Now I am in Medjugorje and my service is to keep the paths of Krizevac and Podbordo clean. At first it was very difficult for me because I felt that I was superior to these tasks. But then I came to understand that for God there are no difficult or easy tasks if we do everything out of love and that my healing is worth any price. In Jesus and Mary, your John Peter".

9.7 CURED OF DRUNKENNESS

My brother-in-law had been given up by the doctors and had refused any spiritual help. At that time, the message of Our Lady of Peace of Medjugorje came to my mind: "Pray, pray with your heart to God and offer Him a sacrifice. We began to pray a lot to the Lord, with Masses, rosaries and other prayers, so that my brother-in-law would be saved and that my husband would stop drinking. After he did not want to talk to the first priest, a second priest came and told him in his ear to offer his terrible sufferings to God; my brother-in-law went to confession and the priest put the scapular of Our Lady of Mount Carmel on him. This happened on Wednesday. Contrary to all the doctors' predictions, he lived three more days when he was given only a few hours to live. My brother-in-law lived until Saturday. A few hours before my brother-in-law died, my husband, who was an alcoholic, was ready to begin full rehabilitation. In fact, my husband stopped drinking after 30 years. I thank the Blessed Virgin for these two great favors. A. M., Guadalajara

9.8 FROM PUERTO RICO

I would like to give a testimony of the experience that two couples from Puerto Rico had during our pilgrimage to Medjugorje during Holy Week last year. On Holy Tuesday, the pilgrims there received an invitation from the visionaries to a prayer meeting at 10:25 p.m. on the Podbordo. Despite the cold and the wind, we gathered around the place of the first apparitions. Our Lady appeared and, through Ivan and Vicka, asked us to pray at the cross for two hours during those days. On Holy Thursday, after breakfast, in a cold and persistent drizzle, we all saw the Krizevac Cross turning dizzyingly; we knelt down to contemplate this fact. Then the 44-ton cross disappeared, and in its place appeared an immense luminous white cross with the Blessed Virgin underneath. We climbed Krizevac in great haste, in spite of the bad weather, to pray there and pour out our hearts. On Good Friday evening, a large black cross appeared on Krizevac, with a beautiful violet glow emanating from its circumference, and a smaller cross with the same characteristics appeared on the right side. This lasted for several minutes. I leave the symbolism of these events to the discretion of the reader, although I think it is clear to me. Isabela, P. R.; January 17, 1989, Dr. José Abreu Elías.

9.9 AFTER 14 YEARS OF MARRIAGE...

In August 1986, I read a book about Our Lady in Medjugorje. At that time I was very sad: after 14 years of marriage I had no children. The doctors had told me that I would never be able to have them. I entrusted myself to Our Lady and began to pray the Rosary every day. After one year of praying the Rosary, the Lord blessed me and I became pregnant. I could not believe it, nor could my husband at first. When I was four and a half months pregnant, the Lord granted me a trip to Medjugorje, which my parents gave me. There I understood the great love of Our Lady for all her children. I was 43 years old when I got pregnant. My baby was born perfectly healthy on August 23, 1988. It was a girl and we named her Mariana and I cannot thank God enough for this miracle of His love. Guadalajara, Jalisco, January 23, 1989, Carmen Ambrosio de Ponce.

CHAPTER 10: THANKS AND FAREWELL

Dear, thank you for coming this far, I am sure that some of my previous paragraphs have brought tears to your eyes. I just want to tell you that now there is something that has awakened in you in a different way and that is the great devotion to Our Virgin Mary. I hope that you will be able to bear witness to many of the things you have read in this book, because in this way you will be able to bring closer to God some people whose faith is still weak.

I hope to see you again in another of my readings.

CHAPTER 11: BIBLIOGRAPHY

Information from the following sources was used in the preparation of this book:

- "Letters to the Friends of Medjugorje" Nos. 33 to 39. Xavier Center. Guadalajara (with Imprimatur of the Vicar General of the Archdiocese).
- "The Fast", by Fr. Slavko Barbaric. -1988
- "Medjugorje and Meditations, Witnesses, Teachings", The Riehle Foundations - 1988.
- "Blue Letter" The Riehle Foundatios, Ohio, U.S.A.
- "Seven years of Apparitions" René Laurentin - 1988
- "Reina de la Paz" - Magazine No.4, No.5.-P, Fco. Panama.
- "Fco. Verar - Panama - 1987.
- "A Thousand Encounters with the Virgin" - Janko Bubalo - Guadalajara, 1987.
- "Apparitions of Our Lady in Medjugorje" -René Laurentin Barcelona, 1987. -Mexico, 1984.
- "The Apparitions of Medjugorje" -Svetozar Kraljevic- Mexico - 1984
- "The Virgin Mary speaks in Medjugorje" - Tiberio Munar-Mexico - 1984
- "Queen of Peace Newsletter" - The Pittsburgh Canter for Peace.
- "Queen of Peace" - Fr. Tomislav Pervan. USA - 1988.

- "The Queen of Peace speaks to the world" - Volunteers of Mary, San Jose Costa Rica, Florida Center for Peace
- Website Medjugorje.ws

THANK YOU AND GIVE YOUR REVIEWS

Thank you for taking the time to read this book. I have prepared it with much dedication and hope that your faith will be strengthened.

Give your review here:

https://www.amazon.com/review/create-review/edit?ie=UTF8&channel=glance-detail&asin=B0CW6D7ZW4

If you liked my book, it is very important to me that you leave a review on Amazon. It will help me reach more people.

Thank you so much. I pray for all my readers every day.

Sincerely,

Sister Anna Garavitt